This is

SOUTH AFRICA

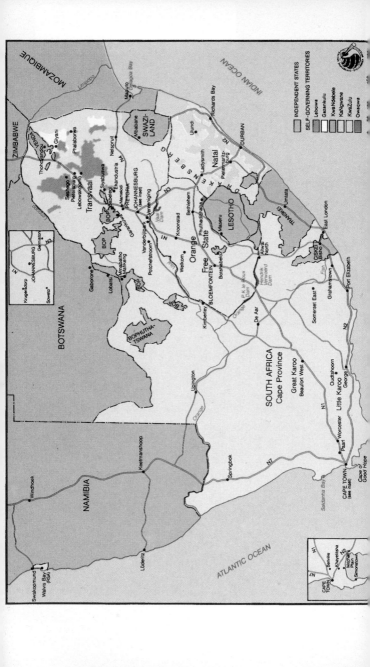

CONTENTS

INTRODUCTION

South Africa is an excitingly diverse country, evident not only in its interesting mix of people and languages, creeds and cultural elements, but also in the nature of the land: its geological formations and regional climates; its mountains, plains and coasts; its fertile farmlands, and its bushveld scrub and arid deserts, each with its own distinctive and often unique plant and animal life.

   This booklet endeavours to provide concise information on the more important aspects of the Republic of South Africa, its people and their achievements. Fur-

Some of the leaders who signed the National Peace Accord, aimed at ending violence, at the Carlton Hotel in Johannesburg on 14 September 1991. From left to right: President F W de Klerk, Dr Nelson Mandela, Dr M G Buthelezi, Dr D R B Madide (Minister of Finance of KwaZulu), Mr J Gomomo (President of Cosatu), and Mr Joe Slovo of the South African Communist Party

ther information is available from the South African Communication Service, Private Bag X745, Pretoria 0001, Republic of South Africa, its regional offices listed at the back of this booklet or the nearest South African diplomatic or consular representative (see *Foreign Relations*).

GEOGRAPHY

Located at the southern tip of Africa, South Africa has a surface area of about 1 127 200 square kilometres (excluding the independent territories of Transkei, Bophuthatswana, Venda and Ciskei). The country is divided into four provinces — the Cape Province (644 060 km^2), the Transvaal (265 470 km^2), the Orange Free State (125 930 km^2) and Natal (91 740 km^2).

The major urban areas are Johannesburg/Soweto/-Randburg, Cape Town/Nyanga/Guguletu, East Rand/-Tembisa/Katlehong, Durban/Pinetown/Inanda, Pretoria/Mamelodi/Atteridgeville, Port Elizabeth/Kayamnandi, West Rand/Roodepoort/Kagiso, Vereeniging/Lekoa/Vanderbijlpark, Bloemfontein/Mangaung and Pietermaritzburg.

Of the 10 self-governing territories that were demarcated in areas historically inhabited by South Africa's various indigenous inhabitants, four are independent

Namaqualand during the flowering season
(Photograph: A Gouws)

today — the republics of Transkei, Bophuthatswana, Venda and Ciskei. The remaining six — KwaZulu, Ka-Ngwane, Lebowa, Gazankulu, Qwaqwa and Kwa-Ndebele — are constitutionally still part of South Africa.

South Africa and the four independent states have been divided into nine development regions, within which a number of 'deconcentration points' (near metropolitan areas) and new 'industrial development points' have been identified (see *Community Development*).

South Africa also encloses the sovereign kingdoms of Lesotho and Swaziland. Flanking the country in the north are, from east to west: Mozambique, Zimbabwe, Botswana and Namibia.

The coastline is nearly 3 000 km long — from Ponta do Ouro on the border with Mozambique in the east to the Orange River in the west. The country's shores are washed by two oceans — the Indian Ocean in the east and the Atlantic in the west. The coastline is swept by two major ocean currents — the warm Mozambique-Agulhas Current that flows from the equator south-wards along the East Coast and westwards along the South Coast as far as Cape Point, and the cold Benguela Current that flows from the Antarctic, north, along the West Coast. The two currents meet at Cape Point.

The topography resembles a narrow-rimmed inverted saucer. The rim, a coastal belt varying in width from 60 km in the west to more than 220 km in the east, adjoins a necklace of mountains marking the edge of the interior plateau. This escarpment is more pronounced in the east and south where it incorporates the country's highest mountain ranges, such as the Drakensberg in the Transvaal and Natal. Some peaks in this range reach heights of more than 3 300 m. The interior plateau is a vast plain with an average elevation of 1 200 m, inter-rupted only occasionally by isolated hills or low ranges.

The subtropical location, straddling 30°S, generally enjoys warm temperatures. Due to the height above sea-level of the interior plateau, temperatures tend to

The Richtersveld in the Northwestern Cape

be lower than in other countries at the same latitude. The increasing elevation towards the northeast also causes temperatures to be fairly even despite a latitudinal span of 13 degrees. Thus the mean annual temperature of Cape Town is 17°C and that of Pretoria (1 600 km northeast) is 17,5°C. East and West Coast temperatures differ sharply, owing to the difference in temperature between the two ocean currents flowing along these shores.

Although temperatures as low as -16°C have been recorded in the eastern mountains, winter is typified by clear skies and sunny days except in the Cape Peninsula. Frost occurs in places from April to October. The average number of sunny days is higher towards the interior as rainfall and cloud cover decreases. In the dry regions of the Northwestern Cape there may be as few as 10 overcast days annually. The average number of daily sunshine hours varies from 7,5 to 9,5 compared with 4,1 in London, 6,8 in Rome and 6,9 in New York.

South Africa is, on the whole, a dry country with a mean annual rainfall of 502 mm, compared with a world average of 857 mm. Rainfall is not only erratic, but also decreases sharply from east to west, from about 1 000 mm annually along the East Coast to less than 200 mm along the West Coast where it can be as low as 50 mm annually. About 65% of the country records less than 500 mm annually — usually regarded as the minimum for successful dry-land crop farming. Along the West Coast and in the Southwestern Cape Province (around Cape Town), rain falls in winter, usually in gentle showers over extended periods. Over the rest of the country most rain falls in short, sharp thunderstorms during summer. Hail is fairly common in the summer rainfall region. Prolonged droughts occur fairly frequently and are often ended by heavy rains and flooding.

Between the winter and summer rainfall regions lies a transitional area where rain occurs in all seasons. This area can be divided into two subregions: a southern coastal belt, and a drier inland corridor behind the mountain ranges.

Fog is common along the West Coast in summer. In the interior it is generally confined to a moist belt along the eastern escarpment. Snow seldom falls beyond the Drakensberg and Maluti ranges, on the eastern escarpment and some coastal ranges.

Perennial rivers are found in only a quarter of the country — the Southern and Southwestern Cape Province and the eastern plateau slopes. Since there are few natural lakes or permanent snowfields, even perennial rivers have a seasonal flow determined by rainfall. In the entire western interior rivers flow only after infrequent storms. The combined run-off of all rivers is 52 000 million m^3 annually — half that of the Zambezi River and about the same as that of the Rhine at Rotterdam. Almost the entire plateau, or approximately 47% of the surface area, is drained by the Orange-Vaal river system. The Orange, the only large river flowing westwards, accounts for only 22% of the total run-off. The well-watered eastern plateau slopes (approximately 12% of the surface area) produce 40% of the total run-off.

Other important rivers include the Vaal (the border between the provinces of the Transvaal and Orange Free State), Limpopo (frontier between the Transvaal and neighbouring Zimbabwe), Tugela (province of Natal), Sundays and Great Fish (Eastern Cape Province), Berg (Western Cape), Letaba (Northern Transvaal), Caledon (Eastern Orange Free State), and several named Crocodile and Olifants in various parts of the country (see *Water*).

With the human settlement of South Africa much of the natural vegetation was either destroyed or replaced by exotic species. Nevertheless, five major communities of indigenous vegetation can still be clearly distinguished

— **Desert and semi-desert:** True desert vegetation occurs in a strip 15 km to 125 km wide along the West Coast — most of Namaqualand. There spring rains allow spectacular carpets of bright flowers — especially the *Mesembryanthemum* (vygie) species and *Compositae* — to bloom almost every year. Karoo or semi-desert vegetation covers most of the western interior. In this area hardy perennial shrubs, often interspersed with low succulents, make good grazing for sheep.

— **Mediterranean:** In the winter rainfall area of the Southwestern and Southern Cape and parts of the South Coast, the Mediterranean-type vegetation consists mostly of evergreen shrubs that have adapted to the rainless summers. Among these are the *Protea* and *Erica* species which have made the wild flowers of the Cape famous throughout the world. Because of the wealth of plant life in this region the area is regarded as one of the six floral kingdoms of the world.

— **Bushveld:** Savannah-type vegetation — dense thornbush, numerous tree (such as the camel-thorn and umbrella-thorn, baobab, fever, marula, acacia and mopani) and shrub species and relatively little grass (usually tall and tufted) — occurs in the far north, northwest and east of the country.

— **Indigenous forest**: Patches of indigenous forest (less than 0,25% of the total surface area) occur along the southern and eastern coastal belts where annual rainfall is regular and exceeds 1 000 mm.

— **Temperate grassland:** Most of the central interior (Orange Free State, Southern Transvaal, Eastern Cape Province beyond the eastern coastal palm belt and Natal) consists of rolling grassy plains and contains few trees (see *Agriculture, Forestry and Fisheries*).

POPULATION

In 1990 the total population of the Republic of South Africa was estimated at 30 797 000. Although blacks, whites, Indians and coloureds are normally distinguished, this does not give a clear picture of the divergent cultural groups which have populated Southern Africa since prehistoric times. If the history and linguistic characteristics of the inhabitants of this area are taken into account, the following groups can be discerned:

The San
The San people or Bushmen are the remnants of an extensive aboriginal population of hunter-gatherers who had roamed over the entire area south of the Zambezi River long before the arrival of the first black peoples. They exhibit distinctive physical characteristics and are at present found in scattered hunting bands in the western parts of Southern Africa.

The Khoikhoin
The Khoikhoin closely resemble the San in physical appearance and in certain cultural characteristics. The two groups are sometimes jointly designated as Khoisan. The Khoikhoin were, however, pastoral people who owned herds of long-horned cattle and flocks of fat-tailed, hairy sheep. The first European settlers at the Cape, encountered scattered groups of Khoikhoin inhabiting the western and southern coastal areas and adjacent hinterland. Eventually they were almost completely assimilated into the coloured population.

The black people
The black population of Southern Africa are the descendants of a variety of essentially Negroid people who

migrated southward into the subcontinent many centuries ago. At present four major groupings can be discerned, viz, the Nguni, the Sotho-Tswana, the Venda and the Tsonga.

The Nguni

At present four major language groups can be distinguished among the Nguni peoples, viz, the Zulu, Xhosa and Swazi-speaking people, and the Ndebele.

The **Zulu-speaking people** are associated with Natal and KwaZulu. Natal/KwaZulu was populated by a variety of autonomous tribes at the beginning of the 19th century. In 1815 Shaka usurped the Zulu throne and then began to reorganise his army. This enabled him to subjugate a group of neighbouring tribes that differed completely from one another, before 1823. A number of tribes fled from the area thus sparking off a period of intense inter-tribal warfare in the interior of Southern Africa. The Ndebele of Zimbabwe and the Shangana of the Eastern Transvaal lowveld are the descendants of the people who fled from Natal during this period under the leadership of Umzilikazi and Soshangana respectively. Shaka was murdered in 1828 and subsequently the Zulu strategy of aggressive expansion gradually diminished.

The **Xhosa-speaking people** who are associated with Ciskei and Transkei can be regarded as descendants of the advance guard of southward migrating black people. They were therefore the first of these peoples to come into close contact with the Khoikhoin and the white frontierfolk in the vicinity of the Kei River. At present the Southern Nguni also include a number of tribes that fled southward into Ciskei and Transkei during the reign of Shaka.

The **Swazi-speaking people** who are associated with the Kingdom of Swaziland and KaNgwane are the descendants of a Nguni group that crossed the Lebombo Mountains from the northeast and started subjugating a number of neighbouring tribes. During the reign of Sobhuza I, the Swazi settled at the present Manzini in

Swaziland. Sobhuza I was succeeded by his son Mswati during whose rule the first contact with whites was made.

The **Ndebele of the Transvaal** can be divided into northern and southern groups. Those in the Northern Transvaal were subject to overwhelming North Sotho cultural identity and language. They are currently found in KwaNdebele and in adjacent areas to the east and northeast of Pretoria. These two Ndebele groups must not be confused with the Ndebele or Matabele of Zimbabwe (see Zulu-speaking people).

The Sotho-Tswana peoples
The **North Sotho**, who are mainly Pedi-speaking, live in Lebowa and the adjacent areas of the Northern Transvaal at present. They comprise a large number of tribes. Some of these tribes were at one stage part of an empire established by the rulers of the Pedi tribe. The Pedi hegemony was, however, destroyed by the Ndebele (Matabele) of Mzilikazi (see Zulu-speaking people). This was followed by a period of extreme dispersal, fragmentation and depopulation until the arrival of the whites when the Pedi chief, Sekwati, succeeded in restoring some order.

The **West Sotho** or **Tswana-speaking peoples**, reside in Botswana, Bophuthatswana, and in parts of the Western Transvaal and Northern Cape. The ancestors of these people arrived from the north in several migrations and as a result of successive struggles they eventually split into a multitude of tribes. This process was aggravated by the depredations carried out by the Ndebele (Matabele) of Mzilikazi (see Zulu-speaking people). When Botswana became a British Protectorate in 1885, it resulted in a further division between Tswana people within and outside that territory.

The **South Sotho** are associated with the mountainous Kingdom of Lesotho, Qwaqwa and the eastern parts of the Orange Free State. Their history can be traced from 1822, when the turmoil created by Shaka in Natal spilt over into the interior of Southern Africa, thus sparking off the period of inter-tribal wars known as the *Di-*

faqane. From their respective mountain strongholds Sekonyela of the Tlokwa tribe and Moshoeshoe I of the Kwena tribe, each established his own empire. Eventually the former was driven away leaving Moshoeshoe I as the ruler of Lesotho. Since 1875, related groups of South Sotho people settled in the adjacent Qwaqwa.

The Tsonga
The **Tsonga-speaking people** originally inhabited the area to the east of the Lebombo Mountains. A part of this group moved westward into the Eastern Transvaal lowveld when Soshangana, the refugee chief from Natal (see Zulu-speaking people), moved into Mozambique with his followers and started to subjugate the local Tsonga population. The empire established by Soshangana in Mozambique eventually deteriorated and since 1894 a considerable number of Shangana people also moved into the Eastern Transvaal lowveld. The inhabitants of this area, known as Gazankulu, are therefore sometimes jointly referred to as Shangana-Tsonga.

The Venda
The **Venda-speaking people** were the most recent black immigrants who settled in the area south of the Limpopo River. They were for some time part of the so-called Monomotapa Empire in Zimbabwe and eventually crossed the Limpopo River into the Soutpansberg Mountains in several migrations. The last of these migrations arrived in approximately 1700 AD. The Lemba, who currently live among the Venda in Venda, are considered to be the descendants of Semitic traders from the East Coast.

The white people
The history of the white people of South Africa dates back to 1652 when the Dutch East India Company established a shipping station at the Cape of Good Hope. In due course the numbers of the first settlers were supplemented by immigrants of mainly Dutch,

German and French extraction. The intermingling of these immigrants eventually resulted in the formation of a distinctive cultural group which eventually became known as Afrikaners. In 1820 a considerable number of British settlers arrived in the territory. About 60% of the whites are Afrikaans-speaking. Both Afrikaans and English are the official languages of the country.

There are also numerous established communities of European extraction — such as from the United Kingdom, Portugal, Germany, the Netherlands, Belgium, Switzerland, Italy, France, Scandinavia and Greece — who speak the two official languages as well as their mother tongue. There is also a well-established Jewish community (mainly English-speaking).

The coloureds

The early population of the Cape was supplemented by a considerable number of slaves from West Africa, Madagascar, India, Indonesia and Malaya. The children produced by these people and the Khoikhoin; people of European origin, and eventually also black people, resulted in the coming into being of the coloured people of South Africa. The coloured people include two subcultural groups — the **Griquas** and the **Cape Malays**. Except for the Malays, most coloureds are Christians and their way of life is unmistakably Western. The majority of coloured people speak Afrikaans. More than 80% of all coloured people reside in the Cape Province.

The Asians

The Asians in South Africa consist mainly of Indians, but also include other smaller groups.

The founding of an Asian community in Southern Africa actually began in 1860 when a considerable number of **Indians** — mainly Hindu from Madras — were brought to South Africa to work as contract/indentured labourers on the Natal sugar plantations. Their numbers were later supplemented by Gujarati-speaking

Muslims. At present more than 80% of all Indians still live in Natal. Most are fluent in English and a small percentage also speak Afrikaans. Their original mother tongues of Tamil, Telugu, Hindi, Gujarati and Urdu are still maintained within the different communities.

Between 1904 and 1906 more than 63 000 **Chinese** labourers were indentured to work in the Witwatersrand goldmines. Although the majority of these people were repatriated since 1907, about 13 000 people of Chinese extraction currently form part of the South African population. The Chinese are fluent in English and often in Afrikaans, while some families still use Cantonese or Mandarin at home.

Immigration

From 1988 to 1990 South Africa attracted about 12 000 immigrants annually while the loss of emigrants was about 5 800 a year. Immigration and emigration figures fluctuated considerably in the first half of the 1980s, due largely to a deep economic recession since 1982 and uncertainty on the part of prospective immigrants about the political future of South Africa. In 1990 the country recorded a gain of 9 777 immigrants (14 499 immigrants and 4 722 emigrants).

In recent years most immigrants have come from Britain, Europe and Africa (especially Zimbabwe). Where a shortage of high level manpower exists, the Department of Home Affairs may, in its discretion, assist such a suitably qualified immigrant and his family to immigrate to the Republic by paying 80% of the passage costs applicable to an adult person from the point of departure in his country of origin to his destination in the Republic.

Urbanisation

The discovery of diamonds and gold in the interior of South Africa, and the industrialisation which followed in its wake, sparked off a process of rapid urbanisation. Large numbers of blacks began to migrate from the rural areas to the rapidly growing mining and industrial centres in order to sell their labour. Although some of them enter into contracts for fixed periods and then return to the rural areas, more than 50% of all blacks are urbanised. The same holds true for the other population groups. (See *Community Development.*)

HISTORY

Early Holocene epoch until about 2 000 years ago: Scattered groups of hunter-gatherers and herders — Stone Age Khoisan — formed the sole populace of Southern Africa for approximately 8 000 years.

Before AD 300: It is accepted that the first route of human migration to South Africa was down the East Coast. Modern evidence indicates that Early Iron Age communities were established in Natal and the Transvaal.

1400s: Khoisan and various black peoples had settled in many parts of South Africa. Diverse cultures, languages and modes of subsistence had developed over thousands of years.

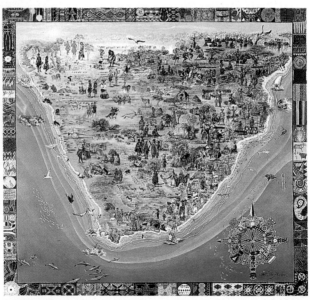

An ethnic map of Southern Africa depicting tribes and customs

(Artist: Charlotte Firbank-King)

1488: Portuguese navigator Bartolomeu Dias sails round the Cape of Good Hope and scraps of information on the local people begin to be recorded. The event marks the beginning of colonial influence over the indigenous Khoikhoin and San.

1497: Another Portuguese seafarer, Vasco da Gama, rounds the Cape on a voyage of discovery to India. During Portugal's century-long dominance of the Cape route, frequent quarrels arose with local people.

1580: Dutchman Cornelis de Houtman, also searching for a passage to the East, arrives in Mossel Bay and trades with the Khoikhoin — the first contact between the Netherlands and the land it was to rule for almost 150 years.

1652: The European movement into the interior starts at the Cape when Jan van Riebeeck reaches Table Bay aboard the *Drommedaris* as Commander of about 90 people sent out on that ship and four companion vessels to establish the Cape outpost.

1688-1700: About 225 French Huguenots — refugees from religious persecution after the revocation of the Edict of Nantes — reach the Cape.

1682: The proclamation of new districts to follow the separation of Stellenbosch from the Cape, recognises movement by farmers into the interior.

1713: A smallpox epidemic devastates the Khoikhoin clans from Table Bay to as far as the Piketberg. The indigenous inhabitants had no resistance to contagious diseases from abroad.

1739: Khoisan resistance to dispossession by advancing frontiersmen leads to a war on the northern frontier of the colony.

1770s: The Xhosa in the Zuurveld to the west of the Fish River encounter the eastward movement of white farmers out to expand their pasturage.

1774 onwards: The frontier colonists and the Khoisan wage war.

1779: A war breaks out on the eastern frontier, the first clash in a continuing series of such skirmishes between whites and blacks later referred to as 'frontier wars'.

1795: The First British Occupation of the Cape — to last until 1803 — takes place to prevent the then Dutch settlement from falling into the hands of France.

1803: Dutch rule is resumed (until 1806) when, in terms of the Treaty of Amiens between Britain and France, the Cape is handed over to the new Batavian Republic.

1806: During Britain's imperial and commercial struggle against her French rival, the Second British Occupation of the Cape takes place.

1814: The Dutch permanently cede the Cape to Britain by means of the London Convention.

1820: The *Chapman* arrives in Algoa Bay with the first wave of about 4 000 British emigrants destined for settlement on the eastern frontier.

Early 1820s: The neutral territory, between the Great Fish and Keiskamma rivers, separating the Xhosa and the colonists on the eastern frontier, breaks down. Small battles begin to take place more often between the colonists and the Xhosa.

1820s and 1830s: The black peoples of Southern Africa experience massive forced migration caused by the bloody rise of the Zulu kingdom. Known in Nguni as the *Mfecane* ('hammering' or 'shattering'), the fighting leaves tracts of land underpopulated or depopulated and the unpleasant results are felt from the Cape to Central and East Africa.

1824: The first white traders and adventurers arrive in Shaka's Zulu kingdom and settle at Port Natal.

1825: Government at the Cape is entrusted to an Advisory Council, although nearly three more decades will pass before meaningful constitutional changes occur.

By 1825: Shaka, king of the Zulus, has created a kingdom that is the most formidable power in Southeast Africa.

1834-1840: Approximately 15 000 Afrikaner frontier-folk abandon the Eastern Cape Colony permanently and embark on the Great Trek northwards into the interior.

1843: Natal is formally recognised as British territory by becoming a district of the Cape Colony.

1848: The Governor of the Cape, Sir Harry Smith, annexes the territory between the Orange and Vaal rivers and the Drakensberg Mountains as the Orange River Sovereignty, thereby strengthening the entire frontier between white and black, from Natal to the Eastern Cape frontier, in British hands.

1852: Britain recognises the independence of the Voortrekker republic north of the Vaal River by the Sand River Convention, which leads to the establishment of the South African Republic (Zuid-Afrikaansche Republiek).

1853: Representative government in the form of the Cape Parliament is instituted at the Cape and meets for the first time in 1854.

1854: The Bloemfontein Convention recognises the independence of the trekker communities between the Orange and Vaal rivers; the Great Trek is concluded. The British Orange River Sovereignty gains independence as the Orange Free State Republic.

1856: The Charter of Natal separates Natal from the administrative authority of the Cape and gives the colony limited representative government.

1857: The visions of a young Xhosa girl, Nongqawuse, leads to the Great Cattle Killing or 'national suicide' of the Xhosa nation. She prophesied that if the Xhosa were to kill all their cattle and destroy their grain, the sun would rise and set again in the east on a given day, and a whirl-wind would sweep all whites and unbelievers into the sea.

1860: The first Indian immigrants arrive in Durban as contract labour for the sugar industry. By 1886 the Indian population of Natal stands at 29 828.

1867: Diamonds are discovered at Hopetown in the Orange Free State Republic.

1870: Diamonds are also discovered at Du Toits Pan near the present Kimberley.

1877: Britain annexes the South African Republic as the colony of the Transvaal.

1880: The first skirmishes in the first Anglo-Boer War in the struggle for Transvaal independence (1880-81) commence at Potchefstroom in the Western Transvaal.

1881: The Transvaal regains its independence after the Pretoria Convention is signed with the British.

1886: Rich gold deposits are discovered on the Witwatersrand by an Australian miner named George Harrison.

1895: Dr Leander Starr Jameson launches the Jameson Raid from Bechuanaland (now Botswana) in an attempt to overthrow the republican government in the Transvaal and bring it into the sphere of British influence.

1899-1902: The republics of the Transvaal and the Orange Free State are formally locked in war with Britain after an ultimatum presented to the British by the Transvaal expires.

1902: The Peace Treaty of Vereeniging, signed at Pretoria, ends the Anglo-Boer War.

The African Political (later People's) Organisation (APO) is founded in Cape Town and comes to represent the interests of the coloured people.

1910: Britain's four colonies in Southern Africa are united in the self-governing Union of South Africa.

1912: The South African Native National Congress (from 1923 to be known as the African National Congress or ANC) is formed in Bloemfontein.

1914: The Union of South Africa, similar to the other members of the British Empire-Commonwealth, is automatically drawn into World War I.

1919: South West Africa becomes a League of Nations 'C' class mandate, which allows for the administration of the territory by the Union of South Africa under its laws.

1920: Colonel (later Sir) Pierre van Ryneveld and Major (later Sir) Quintin Brand of South Africa are the first pilots to fly from Britain to South Africa (45 days from London to Cape Town).

1921: White socialists unite their different organisations to form the South African Communist Party.

1923: The South African Indian Congress is formed.

1925: Afrikaans is recognised as an official language. English is already an official language.

1928: A new national flag (similar to the one still in use) is flown for the first time.

1939: South Africa enters World War II on the side of the Allies.

1945: The South African Prime Minister, Field Marshal J C Smuts, as one of the founders of the United Nations, signs the United Nations Organisation Charter in San Francisco.

1948: The *Herenigde* (Reunited) National Party wins the general election. Over the ensuing years Acts are passed which define and enforce a policy of separate development (apartheid) for racial groups.

1956: The Separate Representation of Voters Act is passed, thereby removing coloureds of the Cape Province from the common voters' roll.

1959: The Pan Africanist Congress (PAC) is established.

1960: The visiting British Prime Minister, Mr Harold Macmillan, makes his 'Winds of Change' speech in the South African Parliament.

Sixty-nine people are killed and approximately 180 wounded when demonstrators surround a police station at Sharpeville, near Vereeniging, and are fired upon by police reinforcements.

The ANC and the PAC are declared prohibited organisations. They go underground and begin advocating the violent overthrow of the government.

1961: The Republic of South Africa comes into existence outside the Commonwealth.

Mr Albert Lutuli, President-General of the ANC, becomes the first African to receive the Nobel Peace Prize.

1967: Professor Chris Barnard performs the world's first heart transplant, at Groote Schuur Hospital in Cape Town.

1974: The UN General Assembly rejects the South African delegation's credentials, depriving the country of its right to participate in Assembly activities.

1976: South Africa involved in Angolan civil war following the precipitate granting of independence by Portugal.

South Africa grants independence to Transkei, the first of its self-governing territories to accept such status.

A protest against Afrikaans as medium of instruction in certain subjects in black schools sparks off trouble in Soweto. The trouble spreads to other black areas in South Africa.

1977: The UN Security Council imposes a mandatory arms embargo against South Africa.

1983: A new constitution provides for a tricameral parliament accommodating whites, coloureds and Indians, while black affairs vests in the State President.

1984: The governments of South Africa and Mozambique sign the Accord of Nkomati, binding themselves to peaceful co-existence.

1990: In a historic opening of Parliament speech on 2 February 1990, President de Klerk announces important steps to abandon the apartheid policy. The African National Congress (ANC), Pan Africanist Congress (PAC), South African Communist Party (SACP) and other organisations are unbanned. Mr Nelson Mandela, the then deputy president of the ANC, is released from prison after 27 years. South Africa's mandate over South West Africa is ended. The Zulu organisation, Inkatha, becomes a political party known as the Inkatha Freedom Party (IFP).

1991: All discriminatory legislation, such as the Group Areas Act and the Population Registration Act, is scrapped.

Legislation is tabled that extends the right of land ownership to all South Africans.

The Government's policy of political reforms leads to improved foreign relations, the gradual lifting of sanctions and the readmission of South Africa to international sport.

The first meeting of Codesa (Convention for a Democratic South Africa) takes place on 20-21 December.

GOVERNMENT

The present South African Constitution provides for a State President; a Parliament consisting of a House of Assembly for the whites, a House of Representatives for the coloureds, and a House of Delegates for the Indians; a Cabinet with the State President as chairman; a Ministers' Council for each House, and a President's Council.

General and own affairs

Fundamental to the system of government is: the distinction made between matters relating only to a specific population group and general or national affairs affecting the interests of all three population groups, and the premise that the three groups have full legislative and executive authority in their own affairs, while assuming joint responsibility for all national affairs.

This means that legislation affecting the affairs of one group only (eg housing) is dealt with by the appropriate House of Parliament without any interference by any other body or person and that Bills on general matters (eg defence) are handled by all three Houses.

The Constitution lays down criteria for distinguishing between 'own' and 'general' affairs. It also allows the State President to decide in consultation with the Cabinet, the Speaker of Parliament and the chairmen of the three Houses whether specific legislation pertains to own or general affairs.

State President

The State President's term of office coincides with the life of a Parliament. That means that he is elected every five years by an electoral college of 88 members appointed by majority vote in the three Houses of Parliament in the following way: 50 by the House of Assembly, 25 by the House of Representatives and 13 by the House of Delegates. The State President is Head of State, Commander-in-Chief of the South African Defence Force and chief executive officer of the Government. However, in exercising most of his more substantive powers, he acts in consultation with the Cabinet, of which he is chairman. The State President may also elect to manage a portfolio for general affairs.

Candidates for the State Presidency must qualify for membership of any House of Parliament but, once elected, the State President may not be a member of a House. He may be removed from office — on the grounds of misconduct or incapacity to perform his functions — by an electoral college constituted in the same way as that by which he was originally elected.

Legislature

Legislative authority is vested in the State President and Parliament.

Parliament

Cape Town is the legislative capital of South Africa and consequently houses the parliamentary buildings. Within Parliament the House of Assembly comprises 178 members. Of them, 166 are directly elected constituencies which have been allocated to the four provinces as follows: the Transvaal 76, Cape Province 56, Natal 20 and Orange Free State 14. The State President appoints one member for each of the four provinces. Eight more are elected by the 166 directly elected members on the basis of proportional representation of the political parties in the House of Assembly.

The House of Delegates consists of 45 members. Of them, 40 are directly elected in 29 constituencies in Natal, eight in the Transvaal and three in the Cape Province. In addition, two more members are appointed and three more indirectly elected in the same way as in the case of the other two Houses.

The House of Representatives consists of 85 members, of whom 80 are directly elected constituencies allocated to the provinces as follows: Cape Province 60, the Transvaal 10, and Natal and the Orange Free State five each. Two members are nominated by the State President while three more are elected by the 80 directly elected members, proportionally according to the strength of the various parties represented in the House of Representatives.

The present Constitution lays down uniform franchise qualifications for all three electorates. This means that all whites, coloureds and Indians who are South African citizens, at least 18 years old and not subject to any of the disqualifications set out in the electoral laws, may register as voters for their respective Houses.

The term of office of a Parliament may not exceed five years. This means that a general election of members of all three Houses must be held at intervals of no more than five years.

The Gallery Hall in the House of Assembly — Parliament, Cape Town

The Constitution lays down only two qualifications for members of Parliament: prospective candidates must qualify to be registered as voters for their respective Houses, and must have lived in the Republic of South Africa for at least five years. Parliament must convene at least once a year and the dates of these sessions are determined by the State President in consultation with the Cabinet.

Legislative process

Legislation on matters affecting the interests of only one population group is dealt with in the appropriate House of Parliament. Bills on own affairs (except money Bills) pass through the following stages: a first reading (which is an introduction of the Bill); referral to a house committee, where it may be amended, and a final second reading (in which the Bill is considered and approved in its final form). The State President must assent to all such Bills passed by a House. A Bill then becomes the law of the country.

Successful legislative procedure in the case of general affairs depends on consensus among the three Houses. This is reflected in the mechanisms provided to promote such consensus on Bills on general affairs. An important mechanism is the joint committees, comprising members of all three Houses. It is their task to seek the greatest possible degree of consensus on Bills and all other issues referred to them by the three Houses.

The Constitution requires that a Bill on general affairs be approved by all three Houses without any material differences before it can be submitted to the State President for his assent.

President's Council

The President's Council consists of 60 members of all three population groups and functions on a part-time basis. Thirty-five of the members are appointed by a majority vote by the three Houses (20 by the House of Assembly, 10 by the House of Representatives and five by the House of Delegates) and 25 are nominated by the State President. Of the last mentioned group, 10 are designated by the opposition parties in the three Houses (six in the House of Assembly, three in the House of Representatives and one in the House of Delegates).

The Constitution limits the term of office of the President's Council to no longer than that of a Parliament and the State President. In practice this means that the Council is reconstituted after every general election for the three Houses of Parliament.

When the three Houses of Parliament are in conflict on a Bill the President's Council may be asked for a decision. If so, it may not amend the legislation, but only recommend that one of the versions of the Bill be submitted to the State President for approval. Alternatively, either of its own accord or by request, the President's Council may merely advise the State President on ways and means of resolving the conflict and reaching consensus. The Council may also advise the State President (that is, the Government) on its own initiative on any issue of national importance other than draft legislation.

Executive authority

The executive authority has two components: the Cabinet consisting of the State President (chairman) and Ministers, who handle general affairs; and three Ministers' Councils, one for each House of Parliament.

Members of the Cabinet may be appointed from the white, coloured or Indian population groups and must be — or must become — members of their respective Houses of Parliament. Members of the three Ministers' Councils must be members of their respective population groups as well as members of the appropriate House of Parliament. The will of the majority parties in the three Houses prevails in their respective Ministers' Councils. The Constitution states that the State President shall designate the member of a Ministers' Council, who in the opinion of the State President has the support of the majority in the House concerned, as the chairman of such Ministers' Council.

The State President can also appoint Deputy Ministers to assist members of the Cabinet and the Ministers' Councils with their duties.

The broadening of democracy

When the Union of South Africa was founded in 1910 the total population included 10 black ethnic groups who by the late 1960s respectively ranged in numbers from a few hundred thousand to four million. Each had — and still has — a territorial base reasonably well-defined by history over more than a century, as well as a cultural identity, including language, and a distinctive socio-political system (see *Population* and *History*). The central question confronting South African governments since 1910 has been the manner in which these 10 black ethnic groups should be democratically fused into the political system.

It had been implicit in the policies of all South African governments, more particularly between the early 1950s and 1985, that the political and constitutional development of black South Africans should be distinct from that of their white counterparts. Over decades statutory foundations had been laid for the separate development of these peoples and their territories to full self-government and, eventually, sovereign independence. Indeed, this 'separate' approach can be traced to the era of British tutelage in the 19th century.

The Development Trust and Land Act of 1936 increased by 6,3 million hectares the land reserved for black occupation in 1913, to bring the total to 15,3 million ha. The Black Authorities Act of 1951 gave statutory recognition to the traditional black political and administrative structures, based on the chief and his counsellors, which were to culminate in a territorial authority based on tribal and regional authorities.

The Promotion of Black Self-Government Act of 1959

formally recognised the various black population groups as distinctive national units and established the constitutional machinery for each to attain self-government and independence. In 1963 Transkei, home of the largest section of the Xhosa people, became the first black territory to reach self-governing status when its territorial authority was replaced by a legislative assembly that has wide-ranging powers.

By the end of 1981 four black territories (Ciskei, Transkei, Bophuthatswana and Venda) with an existing population of 4,7 million had become independent and the remaining six (Lebowa, Qwaqwa, Gazankulu, Kwa-Zulu, KaNgwane and KwaNdebele), with an existing population of 5,3 million, had been granted full internal self-government.

The constitutions of all six of these self-governing territories and the four independent states specify that elections for their legislative assemblies must be held at least every five years. All citizens of these territories — both inside and outside their borders — have the right to vote.

In recent years the foundations have been laid for close functional co-operation between South Africa, Transkei, Ciskei, Bophuthatswana and Venda, and these governments regularly consult on an equal footing on a wide range of issues of mutual concern (see *Foreign Relations*).

Since 1985, however, fundamental policy changes regarding the black communities have been accepted by the Government. Realities have shown that the linkage policy, whereby all blacks — including those living outside the self-governing territories — were ethnically linked to those states, did not satisfy black political aspirations. The Government also stated explicitly that those self-governing territories which did not wish to opt for independence would remain part of South Africa. The Government accepted an undivided South Africa with one citizenship and universal franchise. This means that a new constitutional arrangement, which provides for power-sharing between all groups on a basis of non-domination of one group by another, will have to be negotiated.

The acceptance of the permanency of blacks in what was previously regarded as 'white' South Africa, has already led to dramatic reforms regarding black communities. The system of influx control which restricted the movement of blacks was abolished and the pass system replaced by a uniform identity document for all. In the 1991 parliamentary session legislation was enacted which repealed the Land Acts of 1913 and 1936. Blacks were thereby enabled to acquire full land tenure. South African citizenship has also been restored to blacks residing permanently in South Africa but who, on the grounds of their ethnic origin, became citizens of Transkei, Bophuthatswana, Venda and Ciskei when these states became independent.

The policy of providing for the representation of all communities on all levels of government has already been implemented on the second and third tiers by broadening the base of democracy to include black local authorities in the regional services councils and by including blacks in the provincial executive committees. Provision has also been made for the establishment of joint executive authorities (JEA) between provinces and the self-governing territories for the management of mutual interests. Natal and KwaZulu opted for a JEA.

The most dramatic revision of law was the scrapping of the controversial Population Registration Act which provided for the classification of each citizen in a racial category at birth. The present Constitution which is founded on the same system of classification will remain temporarily in force until a new constitution replaces it. The most important structural issue which therefore remains to be resolved, is the extension of a fully democratic system to central government level. The Government is committed to a negotiated settlement in which all South African voters will share in governing South Africa. Important steps have been taken to facilitate a climate conducive to constructive negotiations. The prohibition on certain political movements such as the African National Congress (ANC), the Pan Africanist Congress (PAC) and the South African Communist Party (SACP), has been abolished, democratic political activities such as protest marches and mass demonstrations have been allowed, and negotiations over a broad political spectrum have been initiated and conducted with the ultimate aim of a completely new constitutional order being drafted by the representatives of the majority of South Africans. It is envisaged that such an order will provide for power-sharing and the protection of human and minority rights.

Second and third-tier government

Apart from the central government, there are the provincial and local levels of government. The Government follows a policy of decentralisation of power to these levels.

Provincial government

Each of the four provinces (the Transvaal, Cape, Natal and Orange Free State) has an Administrator and an executive committee. Each executive committee consists of the Administrator and any number of persons appointed by the State President, giving preference to persons resident in the province concerned. The executive committee is multiracial in its composition.

The administrators and their executive committees are responsible for, inter alia, general matters such as local government, roads, health and nature conservation. They have limited legislative powers in these matters and are accountable to Parliament which must approve each provincial budget annually. The Government is committed to a policy of devolution of power/authority to the lowest possible level.

Local government

The existing system of local government in South Africa provides for separately elected local bodies for the various population groups. These local governmental bodies are empowered to make by-laws and regulations in order to govern their cities and towns. The principal sources of income are rates and taxes, service fees, and subsidies.

At present local government in South Africa is the subject of a major process of restructuring. This process of developing a new non-racial system of local government is part of the national effort to establish a new South African constitutional order through negotiation among all major political groupings.

The results of an investigation into a possible new system for local government served before the Council for the Coordination of Local Government Affairs. The report of the Council as well as the realities of the day compelled a substantial number of local communities to make contact with one another. These realities include

— lack of sufficient sources of income for some local
  authorities
— duplication of services and administrations
— lack of trained and skilled personnel at some local
  authorities

As a result, various local communities started to co-operate on an unofficial basis and to hold talks on co-operation agreements. Some have considered joint decision-making and even the merging of councils.

Legislation did not make sufficient provision for this type of co-operation. Enabling legislation has become a necessity in order to give legal standing to co-operation agreements.

According to the Government's latest report on a new system of local government multiparty congresses or constituent assemblies could be used to negotiate the details of a new metropolitan structure. The report recommends that 66% of votes in a multiparty negotiating group should constitute agreement.

The report is likely to be the subject of negotiations with political parties during constitutional negotiations.

A metropolitan system would have to prevent domination of minorities without being racial or discriminatory. Metropolitan areas will be characterised by a wide range of social and economic classes, a core city surrounded by a number of independent satellite local authorities. Metropolitan government franchise will be non-racial and negotiations will determine the influence of property ownership.

FOREIGN RELATIONS

South Africa's foreign policy is based on its commitment, as described in the preamble to the Constitution,
to seek world peace in association with all peace-loving
peoples and nations. In pursuit of this the country strives
to maintain and promote relations with all nations on
the basis of mutual advantage and respect for one another's sovereignty, including non-interference in
domestic affairs. South Africa maintains diplomatic
and/or consular relations with a host of countries (see
list of cities and telephone numbers at end of chapter).

South Africa and Africa

As an African state, South Africa's overriding con-
sideration is its own interests and the interests of its
fellow Africans, particularly those in Southern Africa
where the country's destiny lies. In the light of this awareness of the common destiny of Southern African states,
the South African Government has undertaken wide-
ranging initiatives to promote co-operation and development in the region. The extensive railway network and
harbour facilities are at the disposal of all states in
Southern Africa as a reliable and efficient channel for
their imports and exports. South Africa's trade with
Africa, excluding members of the South African Customs Union, increased by 24,4% to more than R5 000
million in 1990. Trade with Zimbabwe, Zambia,
Mozambique and Malawi increased by 13,4% to just
more than R3 000 million. The comparable figures for
Lesotho, Swaziland and Botswana are even higher. Although South Africa still has its own underdeveloped
regions, its well-developed economy acts as a catalyst for
general socio-economic development in the sub-equa-
torial region.

There are only a handful of African states that still
refuse any contact with South Africa. During the first 10
months of 1991, no fewer than 65 official delegations

from African states outside Southern Africa visited the Republic of South Africa for bilateral talks.

The South African labour market, especially the mining industry, provides jobs for nearly a million workers from neighbouring countries. The remitted earnings of these workers represent an important contribution to the national income of those countries. South African exports to the rest of Africa exceeded R4 000 million in 1990, 30% more than in 1989. The major exports are manufactured goods and food. In fact, several African states rely on basic food imports from South Africa (see *Agriculture, Forestry and Fisheries*).

Instruments for co-operation have existed between South Africa and its neighbouring countries for many years. Most well known is the Southern African Customs Union. It comprises South Africa, Botswana, Lesotho, Swaziland and Namibia, as well as Transkei, Bophuthatswana, Venda and Ciskei. All member states annually receive substantial revenues from the common customs and excise pool. Other such organisations are the Common Monetary Area, comprising South Africa, Lesotho, Swaziland, Transkei, Bophuthatswana, Venda and Ciskei, which provides for free transfer of funds within the area, free access to the South African capital markets as well as uniform exchange controls; the Southern African Regional Commission for the Conservation and Utilisation of the Soil (Sarccus), founded in 1950, and the Southern African Regional Tourism Council (Sartoc) set up in 1973. The South African Government has given proof of ongoing commitment to co-operation with its neighbouring states. South Africa's ideal is to create conditions for stability in which the human and other resources of the subcontinent can be developed to benefit all the states concerned.

The South African Government believes — a belief shared by responsible local and world leaders — that unhampered international trade and foreign investment in the country will promote government initiatives on the political front towards the creation of a more equitable society. Such initiatives are aimed at achieving full participation by all South Africans at all levels of government.

Several summit conferences involving the heads of government of South Africa, Transkei, Bophuthatswana, Venda and Ciskei have been held in the past and an interstate structure for economic co-operation and regional development has been established.

In addition, several instruments for practical co-operation have come into being. Foremost among these is the Development Bank of Southern Africa with an issued share capital of R2 000 million. The Bank was established towards the end of 1983 after multilateral negotiations lasting more than three years. To promote

During his visit to Kenya in June 1991 President de Klerk held discussions with President Daniel Arap Moi

economic co-operation between South Africa and other African countries, the Economic Co-operation Promotion Loan Fund was established. It is administered by the Department of Foreign Affairs and funded largely by money set aside by Parliament.

On 22 December 1988, after years of meetings and deliberations, South Africa, Angola and Cuba signed formal agreements in New York providing for the United Nations (UN) to implement UN Resolution 435, and for South Africa and Angola to co-operate with the UN in ensuring independence for South West Africa through free and fair elections. On 21 March 1990 South West Africa attained its independence as the Republic of Namibia.

Political reform

The South African Government's political reform programme, which included the legalisation of all political parties and opposition groups as well as the release of political prisoners, led to improved relations between South Africa and the rest of the world.

Under the leadership of State President F W de Klerk, who was inaugurated on 20 September 1989, significant progress has been made towards achieving South Africa's return to full membership of the international community. During May 1990 the State President toured nine European countries where he informed leaders of the irreversible changes that had taken place in South Africa. In October 1990 this was followed by a visit to Britain, Portugal, the Netherlands and Luxembourg. At the end of April 1991 President de Klerk again visited Europe where he was officially received in Britain, Ireland and Denmark. He also visited Morocco on this tour, his first visit to a North African country. President de Klerk paid a state visit to Israel from where he proceeded to the Republic of China. En route he paid a brief visit to Oman and concluded his tour with a state visit to Mauritius. Visits to South America, the Middle East, Moscow and Japan are in the planning stage.

In response to a report on political developments in South Africa released by a UN fact-finding mission in July 1990, UN Secretary-General Dr Javier Perez de Cuellar observed that he had been greatly encouraged by the positive developments that had taken place. Although South Africa has since 1974 been barred from participating in UN activities, there are now various signs of improvement in its relations with the UN.

President de Klerk's official visit to the United States of America in September 1990, during which he had talks with President George Bush, capped the progress made in South Africa's foreign relations. This was a clear indication that the end of South Africa's isolation and sanctions was in sight.

In October 1991 the Commonwealth scrapped 'person-to-person' sanctions with immediate effect and dramatically eased terms for lifting financial sanctions. India, the first country to impose sanctions on South Africa in 1948, ended a ban on direct air links between the two countries as well as cultural and scientific boycotts. Towards the end of the year Japan lifted trade and financial sanctions.

There has also been a noteworthy improvement in South Africa's relations with the Soviet Union and the countries of Central Europe. Links with the former USSR have been resumed with the establishment of interest offices in Moscow and Pretoria in 1991. Consular offices were opened in Romania, Hungary, Bulgaria, Czechoslovakia and Poland. In November 1991 Foreign Minister R F Botha visited the Baltic states and the Ukraine to establish further links.

Relations have also improved with most African states. Within three years South Africa's representation in Africa and the islands has doubled. It has established new missions in the Côte d'Ivoire, Kenya, Morocco, Togo, Madagascar, Mauritius and Angola.

As Africa's most advanced nuclear nation South Africa has made a high profile return to the International Atomic Energy Agency (IAEA). After an absence of 14 years, it participated actively from its seat in the

IAEA's 35th general conference held in Vienna, Austria, from 16 - 20 September 1991.

The return coincided with South Africa's accession to the Nuclear Non-proliferation Treaty and its entering into a safeguard agreement with the IAEA. By taking these two significant steps in rapid succession, South Africa not only considerably strengthened the international non-proliferation commitment, but also paved the way for the establishment of a nuclear weapon-free zone in Southern Africa. The move also signalled South Africa's return to the fold of the United Nations and to multilateral politics in general.

South Africa has diplomatic and/or consular representatives in the following cities (telephone numbers as on 22 November 1991 with dialling codes from South Africa in brackets):

Argentina
Buenos Aires (0954) (1) 311-8991
Comodoro Rivadavia (0954) (967) 26195

Australia
Canberra (0961) (6) 273-2424

Austria
Graz (0943) (316) 37671, 32
Vienna (0943) (222) 326493

Belgium
Antwerp (0932) (3) 31-4960
Brussels (0932) (2) 230-6845

Bophuthatswana
Mmabatho (0140) (3) 2521

Brazil
Belém (0955) (91) 224-8282
Brasilia (0955) (61) 223-4873
Rio de Janeiro (0955) (21) 542-6191
Sao Paulo (0955) (11) 285-0433

Bulgaria
Sofia (0900) (2) 44-2916

Canada
Montreal (091) (514) 878-9231
Ottawa (091) (613) 744-0330
Toronto (091) (416) 364-0314

Chile
Santiago (0956) (2) 231-3361

Ciskei
Bisho (0433) 2-4525

Comores
Moroni 73-1812 via Paris

Côte d'Ivoire
Abidjan (09225) 44-5963

Czechoslovakia
Prague (09422) 73-6174

Denmark
Copenhagen (0945) (3) 18-0155

Finland
Helsinki (09358) (0) 65-8288

France
Le Havre (0933) 22-8181
Lille (0933) 57-5473
Marseilles (0933) (91) 22-6633
Paris (0933) (1) 4555-9237

Germany
Bonn (0949) (228) 8-2010
Bremen (0949) (421) 32-1261
Frankfurt (0949) (69) 719-1130
Hamburg (0949) (40) 41-2961
Hannover (0949) (511) 5-7021
Kiel (0949) (431) 6-8921
Lübeck (0949) (451) 5-7021
Munich (0949) (89) 260-5081
Saarbrücken-Fechingen (0949) (681) 2470
Stuttgart (0949) (711) 32-9933

Greece
Athens (0930) (1) 692-2125
Thessalonika (0930) (31) 516-021/2

Guatemala
Guatemala City (0900) (502-2) 362890, 341531/5

Hong Kong
Hong Kong (09852) 5 77 3279

Hungary
Budapest (0936) (1) 251-2148

Iceland
Reykjavik (09354) (1) 354-1-629522

Israel
Tel Aviv (09972) (3) 695-6147

Italy
  Genoa (0939) (10) 315-129
  Milan (0939) (2) 80-9036
  Naples (0939) (81) 206-931
  Rome (0939) (6) 841-9794•
  Trieste (0939) (40) 44686

Japan
  Tokyo (0981) (3) 265-3366

Kenya
  Nairobi (09254) (2) 228-469 (temporary)

Lesotho
  Maseru (09266) 31-5758

Luxembourg
  Luxembourg (09352) (2) 230-6845

Madagascar
  Antananarivo (09261) (2) 26060

Madeira
  Funchal (09351) (91) 46825/6/7

Malawi
  Blantyre (09265) 62-0444
  Lilongwe (09265) 73-0888

Mauritius
  Port Louis (09230) 212-6925

Monaco
  Monte Carlo (0933) (93) 252426

Morocco
  Rabat (09212) 771-1222

Mozambique
  Maputo (09258) (1) 49-1614

Namibia
  Windhoek (061) 22-9765

Netherlands, The
  The Hague (0931) (70) 392-4501

Norway
  Oslo (0947) (2) 44-7910

Paraguay
  Asunción (09595) (21) 44-4331

Poland
  Warsaw (0948) (22) 41-5501

Portugal
Lisbon (09351) (1) 54-5041
Macau (09853) 77-3279, 77-3463
Madeira (09351) (914) 6825
Oporto (09351) (2) 69-8968

Republic of China
Taipei (09886) (2) 715-3251

Republic of Ireland
Dublin (09353) (353) 930-4488

Romania
Bucharest (0940) (0) 12 0346

Spain
Barcelona (0934) (3) 318-0797
Bilbao (0934) (4) 464-1830, 464-1124
Las Palmas (0934) (28) 33-3394
Madrid (0934) (1) 227-3153

Swaziland
Mbabane (09268) 44651

Sweden
Gothenburg (0946) (31) 131373
Stockholm (0946) (8) 24-3950

Switzerland
Berne (0941) (31) 44-2011
Geneva (0941) (22) 735-7803
Zurich (0941) (1) 911-0660

Transkei
Umtata (0471) 31-2191

Turkey
Istanbul (0990) (1) 175-4793

United Kingdom (UK)
Birmingham (0944) (21) 236-7471
Glasgow (0944) (41) 221-3114
London (0944) (71) 930-4488

Uruguay
Montevideo (09598) (2) 79-0411

United States of America (USA)
Beverly Hills (091) (213) 657-9200/8
Chicago (091) (312) 939-7929
Daphne (091) (205) 438-2145
Houston (091) (713) 850-0150
New York (091) (212) 213-4880
Salt Lake City (091) (801) 266-7867
Washington (091) (202) 232-4400

USSR
Moscow (097) (095) 971-6101

Venda
Thohoyandou (015581) 3-1023

Zaire
Kinshasa (09243) (12) 3-4676

Zimbabwe
Harare (09263) (4) 70-7901/6

International organisations
European Economic Community (EEC)
Brussels (0932) (2) 23-1725

International Atomic Energy Agency (IAEA)
Vienna (0943) (222) 326493 Serie 7

International Monetary Fund & World Bank
Washington (091) (202) 364-0320

United Nations
New York (091) (212) 213-5583
Geneva (0941) (22) 735-7801

Secretariat of the Economic Community of Southern Africa (Secosaf)
Pretoria (012) 341-4313

DEFENCE

The South African Defence Force (SADF) consists of four arms — the SA Army, SA Air Force (SAAF), SA Navy (SAN) and SA Medical Service (SAMS). They are supplemented by the Reconnaissance Regiments and the Chaplain-General's section. The Chief of the SADF and the respective arms of the service also have staff divisions which provide auxiliary services such as personnel, intelligence, logistics, finance and planning. With the exception of the Navy, which is largely composed of Permanent Force members, the Permanent Force element of the Army is relatively small. The SADF comprises mostly national servicemen who undergo one year compulsory military training on reaching the age of 18, members of the Citizen Force, and the Commandos.

Three joint training institutions serve all four arms: the South African Defence College; the Military Academy, where officers read for a B Mil degree, and the College for Educational Technology. In addition, the various arms and certain staff divisions have their own training facilities. Those of the Army are the South African Army College, the South African Army Women's College, the Army Combat School and the various corps training schools (infantry, artillery, armour engineering, signals, personnel, technical services, catering, military police, etc). Those of the Air Force are the SAAF Gymnasium, SAAF College, advanced flying schools, flying schools, airspace control school and a school for logistical training. Those of the Navy are the Naval College, Naval Staff College, *SAS Simonsberg*, *SAS Saldanha, SAS Wingfield* and *SAS Jalsena*. Basic training in the SAMS takes place at the SAMS Training Centre, and advanced training at the SAMS College. Specialised medical activities include the Institutes for Aviation Medicine and Maritime Medicine, and the Military Psychology Institute.

Today South Africa is largely self-sufficient in armaments. In fact, in certain high-technology fields the country has become a world leader.

The Armaments Corporation (Armscor) was established with the aim of making South Africa less dependent on external armaments supplies. Private enterprise was involved from the start. Today Armscor is associated with a large number of private contractors who account for about 70% of the armaments and ammunition manufactured in the country.

In recent years Armscor and the SADF have announced and demonstrated several new, locally developed, weapons systems. These include the 155 mm G5 medium-range gun and its self-propelled version, the G6; the new Olifant main battle tank; new tactical radio systems such as the Ebbehout system; the 127 mm Batelour 40 multiple rocket-launcher, the SAMIL series of military vehicles; the new Darter air-to-air heat-seeking missile capable of detecting, tracking and destroying an enemy target; the mine-resistant Mfezi ambulance, and the ZT3 laser-guided anti-tank missile system.

The pride of the South African Navy is the flotilla of highly mobile strike craft built in South Africa and equipped with several batteries of guided missiles. These craft, as well as the 12 500 ton *SAS Drakensberg* replenishment ship launched in April 1986 have greatly enhanced South Africa's naval capability.

A further major development was the production of the Rooivalk attack helicopter and the Cheetah D and E attack aircraft.

Other innovations include a range of vehicles specifically designed for local conditions. Foremost among these are the Ratel 20, a mechanised infantry-fighting vehicle, the Rooikat armoured car and several mine-protected trucks and personnel carriers, such as the Buffel.

Armscor regularly participates in international armaments exhibitions.

The SADF has a long history of competent service. South African forces served with distinction in the Allied Forces during World Wars I and II and in Korea, and in the Border War in Angola and Namibia (1966-1989). South African pilots also served in the Berlin Airlift of 1948 when they were part of the Allied Forces who supplied food, clothing and fuel to a near-starving West Berlin. South Africa had also been involved in an earlier attempt to bring relief to a beleaguered Warsaw during the war years.

Several dramatic search and rescue operations were carried out by SAAF squadrons in recent years. The large-scale helicopter airlift of all passengers left on deck of the sinking passenger liner *Oceanos* in stormy weather along the Transkei coast in August 1991 earned the SADF respect worldwide. The SAAF's Southern Air Command at Silvermine in fact coordinated the whole rescue operation and no lives were lost. Strike-craft and divers of the SA Navy also assisted during the rescue operation.

Like the SAAF, the SA Navy is often called in to assist in search and rescue operations. During *Operation*

The South African Air Force air ambulance service often helps civilians in emergency situations

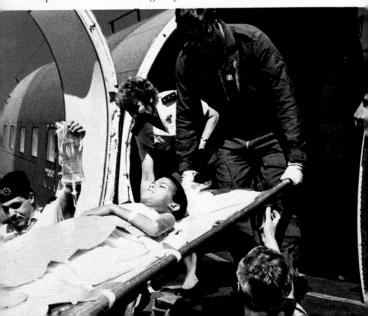

Cashmere in 1990 a South African family, held prisoner by the Renamo rebels in Mozambique, was rescued by a naval task group. *Operation Gillnet* (1990) was the first joint operation by the SA Navy and the Department of Environment Affairs in an endeavour to curb illegal gillnet fishing along the South African coastline. This operation has met with success and convictions have already resulted. In 1990 a SA Navy task group was successfully deployed to help the navy of Zaire to rebuild its naval base at Banana.

Project Curamus, the main functions of which are the treatment, rehabilitation and after-care of the serving as well as veteran handicapped and dependents in the SADF, was launched under the auspices of the SA Medical Service in 1990.

As the fourth largest owner of land in the RSA the SADF is also deeply involved in the protection of the environment. Its Ecological Services Section has a number of interrelated functions, including ecological planning, environmental management and the formulation of long-term conservation strategy. The SADF also proceeded with the registration of several areas as nature heritage conservancies. Several competitions are held annually and trophies are awarded for achievements in Nature Conservation, Environmental Conservation and Environmental Education.

JUSTICE

South African law consists of common law, based on Roman-Dutch law — the latter introduced to the Cape of Good Hope by the Dutch settlers in 1652 — and legislation, parliamentary as well as subordinate, promulgated by various legislative bodies. After the second British occupation of the Cape in 1806, Roman-Dutch common law was retained, but thereafter British law influenced South African law to a degree.

The judicial authority, independent of both the legislative and executive branches of the State, is vested in the Supreme Court, magistrate's courts, including regional courts, and small claims courts, where minor civil disputes are settled.

The Supreme Court
The Supreme Court consists of six provincial and three local divisions. The provincial divisions are the Cape of Good Hope (with its seat in Cape Town), Eastern Cape

The Transvaal Supreme Court, the Palace of Justice, on Church Square in Pretoria

(Grahamstown), Northern Cape (Kimberley), Orange Free State (Bloemfontein), Natal (Pietermaritzburg) and the Transvaal (Pretoria). These divisions are presided over by a Judge President and as many judges as the State President may determine. The local divisions are the Witwatersrand (Johannesburg), Durban and Coast (Durban) and Southeastern Cape (Port Elizabeth) and are presided over by judges of the provincial division concerned. Circuit courts are itinerant local divisions which periodically visit other centres in a particular provincial division. All crimes may be tried by a single judge, but two assessors must be appointed in cases where the death sentence will probably be imposed. The judge may also appoint one or two assessors if he deems it necessary, for example in complicated commercial cases. Trial by jury was abolished in 1969. Ad hoc superior courts of three judges may be constituted to try offences relating to state security, the maintenance of public order or cases involving difficult legal questions.

The highest court is the Appellate Division of the Supreme Court with its seat in Bloemfontein. It is presided over by the Chief Justice and 11 judges of appeal. Its judgments and orders apply to the areas of all other divisions of the Supreme Court and the lower courts.

South African judges are not politically appointed, as for example the judges in the USA. Judges and acting judges are appointed by the State President on the advice of the Cabinet and may not be removed from office except by the State President. This happens only upon an address from each of the respective Houses of Parliament on the grounds of misbehaviour or incapacity.

Lower courts

The lower courts are regional magistrate's courts, magistrate's courts, children's courts, maintenance courts and small claims courts. South Africa is divided into 268 magisterial districts, each with a magistracy presided over by a magistrate, who is appointed by the Minister of Justice. A magistrate may try both criminal and civil cases. In criminal cases a sentence of imprisonment not exceeding 12 months, a fine not exceeding R4 000, correctional service, community service or a warning may be imposed, except where there are prescribed statutory provisions regarding sentencing, as for example in the case of drug trafficking. In civil cases the magistrate's jurisdiction is limited to claims involving no more than R20 000 (R50 000 in case of liquid documents). In 1990 the 309 magistrate's offices had a complement of 822 magistrates, 993 prosecutors and 5 704 officials of other ranks.

The country is divided into seven regional areas where **regional courts** hear only serious criminal cases and may impose sentences of, inter alia, imprisonment not exceeding 10 years or fines not exceeding R40 000. A criminal case in the Supreme Court is sometimes preceded by a preparatory examination in a magistrate's court. More often, though, in such cases the accused only pleads to the charge in the magistrate's court whereafter it is transferred to the appropriate trial court. Statutory provision has been made for the appointment of assessors in regional courts as well as magistrate's courts.

Provision is made by the Inquest Act of 1959 for the holding of a **judicial inquest** in the case of a death or alleged death, apparently due to causes other than natural. Although an inquest is usually held by the magistrate of the district in which the death is alleged to have occurred (if criminal proceedings are not instituted in connection with the death), provision is now also made for the holding of an inquest by a judge or regional magistrate.

The **children's court** hears cases concerning the safety and well-being of children. In larger centres, a magistrate's court is sometimes set aside to deal exclusively with cases in which the accused are under the age of 18 years.

As its name implies, a **maintenance court**, which is a

specialist section of the magistrate's court, enforces maintenance orders originating in South Africa or in other countries designated for this purpose by the State President. These courts are also competent to order the payment of maintenance.

The **small claims court** has jurisdiction in certain small civil claims of up to R 2 000 in value. The presiding officer in such a court is a commissioner who is appointed from the ranks of the legal profession and renders his or her services free of charge. No legal representation is allowed and the commissioner questions both parties. The commissioner's ruling is final and there is no appeal to a higher court. There are 97 of these courts in operation. This court ensures justice through swift and simple procedures.

Family advocate

In terms of the Mediation in Certain Divorce Matters Act of 1987, family advocates may be appointed at each division of the Supreme Court of South Africa. The family advocate is charged with the duty of assisting the Supreme Court in divorce actions involving the interests of minor children, and in applications for the amendment, rescission or suspension of an existing order with regard to the custody or guardianship of, or access to, a child. A pilot project was launched at the Transvaal Provincial Division of the Supreme Court during September 1990 and extended to the Witwatersrand Local Division on 1 May 1991. Further extension is planned for 1992.

Special courts

Black citizens have access to both magistrate's courts and the Supreme Court, but special courts are also provided where disputes are settled in terms of traditional law and custom. Thus, a local chief or headman may be authorised to decide in terms of indigenous law and custom such civil claims as one black person may bring against another. Proceedings in such courts are informal and no written record is kept. An appeal against a judgment in these courts can be heard by a magistrate's court. A magistrate's court may apply either common law or indigenous law in respect of certain actions between blacks.

Provision is also made for special black divorce courts. Special courts to deal with a process of alternative dispute resolution were recently instituted to deal with disputes by obviating the use of strict and formal procedures of the traditional judicial forums.

Legal practitioners

The legal profession is based on the British system and consists of a Bar and a Side Bar. Advocates are members of the Bar and enjoy a right of appearance in the respective divisions of the Supreme Court as well as the lower courts, but attorneys represent clients only in the lower courts. Advocates are not directly engaged by litigants, but are briefed by an attorney.

An attorney gives legal advice to clients and also advises them on various other matters. The attorney may also be qualified to act as a notary or a conveyancer who prepares deeds of transfer and certificates of title. The minimum qualification for admission as an advocate is the 5-year LL B degree; the B Proc degree for admission as an attorney; the Diploma Iuris for appointment as a magistrate, and the B Iuris degree for admission as a state prosecutor.

State attorneys have the same qualifications as those in private practice and are appointed by the Minister of Justice to render legal services to the State. State law advisers furnish the various government departments and provincial administrations with legal advice and draft Bills to be presented to Parliament. Attorneys-General are appointed by the State President from among the ranks of State advocates to direct public prosecutions in their respective areas of jurisdiction.

Statutory bodies

The Legal Aid Board was established in 1969 to provide legal aid for indigent persons or litigants. In an attempt to establish a broader base of legal representation for the public, a system is at present being introduced whereby persons (known as 'public defenders') who have training and experience in defending criminal cases, and who will be available on a constant basis, will represent undefended accused persons in criminal cases. The Legal Aid Board is responsible for the administration of the public defender system.

The South African Law Commission, comprising two judges of appeal, two full-time members and various other experts, was established by the South African Law Commission Act of 1973 to do research on South African law and to recommend measures of reform to suit changing circumstances. This ensures a scientific and methodical process of law reform. The members of the Commission are appointed by the State President. The Commission is assisted in the performance of its functions by a team of full-time researchers and administrative personnel.

Bill of Rights
A Bill of human rights, justiciable by an independent judiciary and an essential part of a future South African constitution, will ensure the recognition and protection of individual rights in respect of race, culture, sex, language, religion and social class.

These are among the recommendations included in the interim report of the South African Law Commission on group and human rights, released on 2 November 1991. In the report recommendations are made regarding a variety of individual and group rights. First, second and third generation rights, or so-called blue, red and green rights, are examined.

First generation or blue rights recognise, among other things, the individual's right to life. It is recommended that freedom of speech, the freedom to engage in science and art, freedom of movement, and freedom to assemble peacefully and unarmed must be recognised. Every individual has the right to freedom of association.

Regarding children's rights free, state education for

the primary school phase is proposed. Schools and training institutions may not discriminate on the grounds of race, religion or ethnic origin. However, private schools and institutions may reserve the right of admission.

The report also recommends protection of private ownership. Equality before the law must be protected, guaranteeing the right to exercise the vote on a basis of equality and the right to form political parties.

Second generation or red rights are mainly protected in a 'negative' manner in the Bill, which means that the State may not encroach upon certain socio-economic rights. Employees have the right to strike and to bargain collectively, and may not be subjected to unfair labour practices. In turn, employers may apply the principle of no work, no pay in terms of the law.

Third generation or green rights protect the right of each individual to live in a clean environment and to the protection and conservation of the environment.

Several articles in the draft proposals detail the setting up of a special Constitutional Chamber of the Appellate Division to hear appeals against judgments involving issues arising from the Bill of Rights, and the setting up of a Human Rights Commission to educate people on the Bill, to investigate amendments and to appoint an **ombudsman** to act on behalf of individuals and organisations who feel their constitutional rights have been violated by state agencies.

The ombudsman will also act as a mediator. He will try to achieve settlement between an aggrieved party and the body who has allegedly been in breach of the Bill of Rights. He will have to report once a year to the Government.

South African Police

The South African Police (SAP) was established as a National Police Force in 1913. The Police Act of 1958 stipulates police duties as follows:

— to preserve the internal security of South Africa

— to maintain law and order
— to prevent crime
— to investigate offences and alleged offences.

In order to bring about greater efficiency in the Force, the Police Force has recently been divided into four divisions and as from 1 August 1991 the structure of the Force is as follows:

— Division: Visible Policing
— Division: Crime Prevention and Investigation
— Division: Human Resources Management
— Division: Auxiliary Services

An Endangered Species Protection Unit has been formed to combat poaching and illegal practices involving wild animals.

Child protection units are based in all the regions.

The mission of the SAP reads as follows: 'We undertake, impartially and with respect for the norms of the law and of society, to protect the interests of the country and everyone therein against any criminal violation, through efficient service rendered in an accountable manner'.

In order to ensure impartial policing, all police are prohibited by law from enrolling as members of any political party.

At present the SAP is one of the institutions which already makes use of the most advanced methods and techniques in all fields. Members of the Force have been made well aware of the changing circumstances in South Africa which will result in higher demands being made on the Police. Consequently, intensive research concerning the controlling of crime has already commenced and the first comprehensive report is now available.

The SAP's basic training colleges are located in Pretoria, Hammanskraal near Pretoria, Bishop Lavis in Cape Town and Chatsworth in Durban. Advanced training is catered for at the SA Police Academy in Graaff-Reinet, the College for Advanced Training in Paarl and the Management Development Centre at Silverton in Pretoria.

Department of Correctional Services

The task of the Department of Correctional Services is 'to promote community order and security by exercising control over, detention of and dealing with prisoners and persons under correctional supervision in the most cost effective and least restrictive manner'.

The Department's headquarters is the policy-making body and regional commissioners coordinate the activities in their regions. The executive level comprises commanding officers and heads who are in control of the prisons.

There are 200 prisons countrywide which include 16 prison farms.

The department has a staff of approximately 23 000.

The detention and physical care of prisoners is the most important responsibility of the management of all prisons. A high standard of health care and hygiene is maintained in all prisons according to internationally accepted norms.

A variety of programmes are made available to sentenced prisoners to promote their eventual successful reintegration into society.

The provision of education includes literacy tuition as well as primary, secondary and tertiary education and preparedness and recreation programmes.

The performance of labour by and the training of prisoners not only keep prisoners constructively and sensibly occupied during their detention, but also better equip individuals to return to the community to lead an independent and productive life after their release.

Social work services, which are mainly rendered by means of case work and group work, are aimed at the effective social functioning (role fulfilment) of the prisoner while he is in prison and also after his release.

The psychological service has as its aim the provision of psychological treatment to convicted prisoners, as required, in order to maintain or improve the mental health of those prisoners.

Church and religious groups are encouraged to minister to their members/followers who are in prison.

In addition to persons detained in prisons, the Department also manages a system of probation, locally known as correctional supervision, where persons serve their entire sentences within the community under the supervision of correctional officers in the employ of the Department.

ECONOMY AND FINANCE

The South African economy, based almost entirely on agriculture until about a century ago, was transformed virtually overnight by the discovery of diamonds in 1867 and the world's richest gold reefs on the Witwatersrand in 1886 (see *Mining*). For the next 60 years until 1945 mining was the greatest single source of national income. World War II, which had completely disrupted traditional foreign sources of supply, boosted local manufacturing to such an extent that secondary industry soon emerged as the major contributor to the gross domestic product (GDP), a position it still holds.

In 1990 the GDP amounted to about R 235 000 million. The most important contributions were made by manufacturing (R 60 000 million), mining (R 25 100 million), commerce (R 31 700 million), transport and communications (R 19 300 million), agriculture (R 11 900 million) and electricity, gas and water (R 10 800 million). (See *Energy*, *Agriculture*, *Forestry and Fisheries*, *Water*, *Mining*, *Industry*, *Foreign Trade*, *Industrial Relations*, *Transport* and *Communications*.)

As is pointed out in *Foreign Trade*, the reciprocal flow of goods and services between South Africa and its trading partners represents a greater proportion of the GDP (47,0% in 1990) than in the case of most other countries. The economy is therefore very sensitive to international recessions and general conditions in the major Western industrialised countries, which buy most South African exports. It passes through fairly regular cycles of upswings and downturns in sympathy with economic conditions prevailing in the West. Thus, the real growth rate varies considerably according to the state of the business cycle, as the following figures show: 1980 (6,6%), 1981 (5,4%), 1982 (-0,4%), 1983 (-1,8%), 1984 (5,1%), 1985 (-1,2%), 1986 (0,2%), 1987 (2,1%), 1988 (4,1%), 1989 (2,1%) and 1990 (-0,9%).

In 1990, South Africa's gross national product per capita at current prices amounted to R6 788. In an international comparison made among 124 countries and using 1988 figures, South Africa's gross national product per capita in US dollars, ranked 41st. It was, however, approximately seven times higher than the average per capita income for the countries in sub-Saharan Africa, excluding South Africa.

In recent years the economy has also been plagued by an unusually high inflation rate which inhibited growth and undermined the competitive ability of South African industry on world markets. According to the official consumer price index, the average annual inflation rate was 2,8% for the period 1960/70, but then accelerated to an annual average of 10,6% from 1970 to 1980 and 14,7% from 1980 to 1990. The problem of high inflation is receiving the urgent attention of the Government. The Economic Advisory Council recommended a strategy for bringing down the inflation rate and the Government started implementing these recommendations early in 1988. Essential measures outlined in the report include monetary and fiscal discipline, various new policies to promote effective competition, and a consistent and restrained policy approach by the Government towards wages and prices under its control. During the past two years monetary policy has purposefully been applied with the prime objective of curtailing inflation.

A study conducted in 1991 by the Union Bank of Switzerland compared 48 cities and found Johannesburg to be the 14th least expensive. The survey compared the relative prices of a 'basket' of 112 goods and services. From an international point of view, South Africa, although becoming more expensive over the past three years, remains a relatively inexpensive country in which to live.

Private enterprise

The economy is based on private enterprise and ownership, and a free-market system, and in recent years the Government has formally recommitted itself to such a system. In 1979, 1981 and 1986 it arranged three public conferences with South African business leaders during which it laid the foundations for a development partnership between the public and private sectors in which the former provides the physical and social infrastructure, and the latter combines production elements to produce real wealth.

In terms of this renewed commitment, the Government is scaling down its role as entrepreneur and supplier in the market place. On occasion in the past, whenever private enterprise was reluctant or lacked the resources to launch a project considered essential for economic development, the State stepped in as developer or entrepreneur. Examples of successful state enterprises are the oil-from-coal plants Sasol 1, 2 and 3, steel giant Iscor, electricity utility company Eskom, Foskor (Phosphate Development Corporation) and Alusaf (Aluminium Corporation of South Africa). This policy will still be applied whenever necessary, but maximum privatisation remains the ideal. In this spirit the public has already been given the opportunity to buy shares in Sasol and Iscor.

Development Bank of Southern Africa
The Development Bank of Southern Africa (DBSA) was established in 1983. It provides loan finance, preparation assistance, technical assistance and grants for economic development projects to Southern African national, regional and local governments, their development agencies and non-government organisations involved in development.

On 31 March 1991 the Bank had 1 301 projects in the pipeline and had a total number of fixed commitments of 760 projects towards which it expected to make a total financial contribution of an estimated R5 000 million.

Development corporations
Another instrument for economic development in South Africa is the Small Business Development Cor-

poration (SBDC) which was established in 1981 as a joint venture of the public and private sectors. It provides loans and advisory services to smaller businesses. The equity of the SBDC is divided equally between the Government and the private sector, but it is managed according to business principles as the voting rights on the board of directors are controlled by the private sector.

Since its inception in 1981 the Corporation has:
— granted more than R 1 260,3 million in loans to about 34 000 entrepreneurs
— developed property projects to the value of R 300 million, covering lettable premises of more than 748 642 m^2
— created job opportunities for more than 279 100 people at a cost of R3 700 per job opportunity
— assisted more than 1 200 000 people with information and advice since 1 April 1984. It receives approximately 18 000 enquiries monthly.

Because the Government considers the development of small business a vital element in its general economic strategy, it supports various small business institutes which render training and consultation services to small entrepreneurs.

The close corporation as a form of enterprise was established in January 1985 and satisfies the requirements of the small entrepreneur. By 31 July 1991, 205 000 close corporations had been incorporated, of which an estimated 37 000 had previously been companies.

Foreign investment
South Africa has traditionally provided lucrative investment opportunities for foreign financiers and industrialists. By the end of 1988 total foreign investment had reached over R 70 000 million — about 60% of this was accounted for by Europe and 26,9% by the Americas.

Returns on investments in South Africa have consist-

Personal income tax scales for the 1991/92 fiscal year

Taxable income	Unmarried			Married					
				No children			Under 65		
	Under 62	62-64	Over 65	Under 62	62-64	Over 65	1 child	2 children	3 children
10 000	0	0	0	0	0	0	0	0	0
11 000	135	15	0	0	0	0	0	0	0
12 000	345	225	0	0	0	0	0	0	0
13 000	555	435	0	170	50	0	70	0	0
14 000	765	645	0	360	240	0	260	160	60
15 000	975	855	0	550	430	0	450	350	250
16 000	1 225	1 105	0	760	640	0	660	560	460
17 000	1 475	1 355	0	970	850	0	870	770	670
18 000	1 725	1 605	0	1 180	1 060	0	1 080	980	880
19 000	1 975	1 855	0	1 390	1 270	0	1 290	1 190	1 090

	2 225	2 105	125	1 600	1 480	0	1 500	1 400	1 300
20 000	2 225	2 105	125	1 600	1 480	0	1 500	1 400	1 300
25 000	3 675	3 555	1 575	2 750	2 630	650	2 650	2 550	2 450
30 000	5 325	5 205	3 225	4 050	3 930	1 950	3 950	3 850	3 750
35 000	7 125	7 005	5 025	5 500	5 380	3 400	5 400	5 300	5 200
40 000	9 075	3 955	6 975	7 100	6 980	5 000	7 000	6 900	6 800
45 000	11 075	10 955	8 975	8 850	8 730	6 750	8 750	8 650	8 550
50 000	13 125	13 005	11 925	10 750	10 630	8 650	10 650	10 550	10 450
55 000	15 225	15 105	13 125	12 700	12 580	10 600	12 600	12 500	12 400
60 000	17 365	17 245	15 265	14 700	14 580	12 600	14 600	14 500	14 400
65 000	19 515	19 395	17 415	16 750	16 630	14 650	16 650	16 550	16 450
70 000	21 665	21 545	19 565	18 800	18 680	16 700	18 700	18 600	18 500
75 000	23 815	23 695	21 715	20 900	20 780	18 800	20 800	20 700	20 600
80 000	25 965	25 845	23 865	23 000	22 880	20 900	22 900	22 800	22 700
100 000	34 565	34 445	32 465	31 600	31 480	29 500	31 500	31 400	31 300
150 000	56 065	55 945	53 965	53 100	52 980	51 000	53 000	52 900	52 800

Source: Department of Finance

The Johannesburg Stock Exchange

ently been competitive and the country's credit-worthiness has always been good (1991: 36th in the Euromoney Risk rankings). Over the past years, however, the investment climate has been greatly influenced by socio-political developments. Occurrences such as the social unrest, the state of emergency, and disinvestment and economic sanctions have deleteriously affected foreign perceptions of the domestic, political and economic outlook. Debatable as these perceptions might be, they resulted in a withdrawal by foreign banks of credits to South African banks and other business enterprises and the imposition on 1 September 1985 of a 'standstill' on the repayments due on the major part of the country's foreign debt. However, since the debt 'standstill' until the end of 1990, more than $7 300 million of foreign debt has been repaid.

Due to positive developments over the past two years, much foreign confidence in South Africa has been restored, sanctions lifted and investments increased.

Fiscal policy

Conservatism has been a hallmark of the fiscal policies of all South African governments. As far as possible, all current expenditure by the central government is covered by current revenue and all deficits are financed in the least inflationary manner.

The chief sources of revenue are income tax and indirect taxes, such as value added tax and customs and excise duties. Income tax rates for individuals and companies are determined in the national budget approved annually by Parliament. These rates are sometimes supplemented by surcharges and loan levies, the latter being repayable with tax-free interest. Other direct income taxes include taxes on dividends accruing to non-residents and taxes on the undistributed profits of companies, royalties and donations, and estate duty.

The accompanying table (see overleaf) shows the income tax payable by individuals in 1991/92. In 1991/92 Standard Income Tax on Employees (Site) will apply to all net remuneration of up to R50 000 for all employees. If an employee's salary exceeds the Site ceiling of R50 000, a Pay-As-You-Earn system (Paye) is also applied. Companies are divided into four groups for tax purposes. Gold-mining companies pay according to a formula which increases with the profitability of the mine. Diamond-mining companies pay 48 cents in the rand plus a surcharge of 6% (in 1991/92) thereof and other mining companies pay 48 cents in the rand plus a surcharge of 6% (in 1991/92). All other companies pay 48 cents in the rand (in 1991/92). Insurance businesses will pay 43 cents in the rand in 1991/92.

The main forms of indirect tax are customs duties levied on a wide range of imports, excise duties collected on commodities such as liquor, tobacco and other luxury goods, a fuel levy, and a value added tax of 10% on virtually all goods and services.

South African Reserve Bank
The South African Reserve Bank is the central bank of South Africa and has as its aim the protection of the domestic and external value of the rand. It acts as banker, agent and adviser to the central government and provincial administrations; formulates and applies monetary policy; issues banknotes; concludes national and international transactions, including the purchase and sale of foreign exchange; keeps all cash reserves which registered deposit-taking institutions must maintain with it, and buys and sells the output of all gold-mines.

Other institutions
Other public financial institutions are the Land and Agricultural Bank which provides financial assistance to farmers and agricultural co-operatives; the Corporation for Public Deposits which accepts call deposits from public institutions and invests it in bills, government and other public stock; the Public Investment Commissioners who manage and invest in government and other securities, those trust and deposit funds which the Government and public organisations are obliged to hold with them, and the Post Office Savings Bank which accepts deposits in various forms from the public, mainly to be used as loan capital for the recently privatised Posts and Telecommunications companies, where the Government is the sole shareholder.

Private financial institutions
South Africa has well-developed money and capital markets. After World War II the private financial institutions were expanded and developed on a large scale to meet the needs of a rapidly expanding economy.

These institutions, under ever-increasing competition, have improved and expanded their services continually over the past few years. Thus, an extensive network of automatic teller machines (ATMs) and futures and options markets have been developed.

A major change to the financial structure in South Africa was the passing of the Deposit-taking Institutions Act of 1990 which came into operation in February 1991. Its aims are to level the 'playing field' of the deposit-taking institutions and to secure a more stable financial structure in South Africa. By the middle of 1991, there were 64 registered deposit-taking institutions (the previously named commercial banks, merchant banks, discount houses, general banks and building societies) specialising in retail banking, corporate banking, mortgage finance and institutions providing one-stop combinations of these services. Total assets of deposit-taking institutions exceeded R 220 billion by mid-1991.

The insurance business is also well developed. In 1989 there were 88 registered insurance companies with assets totalling R 133 000 million. Thirty-seven of them undertake only long-term insurance, 14 both long-term and short-term business and 37 only short term. In 1989 there were 13 507 private pension and state controlled funds with assets of R 46 793 million, and 37 participation mortgage bond schemes.

The market value of ordinary company shares quoted on the Johannesburg Stock Exchange (JSE) was R 429 billion at the end of December 1990. During 1990, 2 623 million shares valued at about R 24 000 million changed hands. The nominal value of the first-class bonds traded on the JSE in 1990 was in the region of R 240 000 million. Measured in terms of market capitalisation, the JSE, at the end of 1990, was the 14th largest exchange of its kind in the world.

AGRICULTURE, FORESTRY AND FISHERIES

Agriculture

Conditions in South Africa are generally unfavourable for agriculture. The country is relatively dry, rainfall is unreliable, severe droughts occur frequently and according to world standards South Africa has a fairly limited amount of land with high agricultural potential.

Of the 14 million hectares suitable for crop production, only about three million hectares are considered to have a high potential. A variety of restrictive ground factors such as shallowness, density, acidity, deficient nutritive value, alkalinity, unfavourable structure, and intermittent and poorly dispersed rainfall contribute to the suboptimal potential of about 82% of arable land. About 20% of the surface area is potentially highly erosive and the degree of erosion which alternates between negligible and extreme, depends on the effect of environmental factors.

Agricultural production has nonetheless almost doubled over the last 20 years. Indeed, South Africa is one of a few net food exporting countries.

South African agricultural exports have become important to many countries in sub-Saharan Africa. The most important exports are animal products, vegetable products, prepared foodstuffs as well as beverages. Consignments of fresh and canned fruit, canned meat, baby foods, powdered milk, maize products and various flours are regularly railed to this area (see *Foreign Relations*).

In 1960 agriculture contributed R615 million (or 12,5%) to South Africa's gross domestic product (GDP). By 1990 the share of agriculture in the GDP had declined to 4,8%. Over the past few decades the number of farms has decreased from 77 000 to under 60 000.

Nevertheless, the gross value of agricultural production was R 20 702 million in 1990 compared with R 20 125 million in 1989, R 17 111 million in 1988 and R 14 733 million in 1987. The net income of farmers decreased from R 6 700 million in 1989 to R 5 400 million in 1990. Production costs have risen sharply. In 1990 the cost of the main inputs (fuel, fertilisers, packing materials, feeds, dips and sprays, and maintenance) increased by about 11,6%. More than one million people (mostly blacks and coloureds) make a living from the agricultural industry, that is excluding the employment of migrant labourers.

Climatic conditions vary from subtropical through Mediterranean to semi-desert and allow the production of an impressive array of crops. Cattle (for beef and dairy products), sheep (for wool and mutton) and goats (for mohair and meat) are also successfully reared and grazed. Because the country is relatively dry many crops are grown under irrigation. By 1991 approximately 1,2 million ha had been put under irrigation.

Maize is planted on 40% of the 8 675 000 ha cultivated annually. In the 10 years 1968-1978 the crop was virtually doubled due to improved methods of cultivation and the introduction of high-yield cultivars adapted to local conditions. Today rainfall largely determines the size of the crop. The 1989/90 crop was 8,3 million tons with a gross value of R 2 400 million.

Other major crops are wheat (two million tons in 1989/90), grain sorghum (288 000 tons), groundnuts (68 000 tons), sunflower seed (628 000 tons), sugar-cane (18,6 million tons), fruit — deciduous, citrus and subtropical (2,1 million tons) — and vegetables (1,8 million tons). In good years South Africa produces sufficient quantities of all these crops to meet its domestic requirements and to export varying volumes. South African wines are exported to more than 25 countries, but 90% of production is consumed locally. The gross value of the 1989/90 fruit harvest was R 1 597 million.

South Africa is also an important producer of meat (884 000 tons of red meat and 563 000 tons of poultry meat in 1989/90), hides and skins, wool (105 200 tons) and milk (2,4 million litres annually). Due to a severe drought during the early 1980s the cattle and sheep herds declined. However, since 1988 these herds have again increased. In 1990 cattle numbered 8,7 million and sheep 30,0 million. The number of pigs remained fairly constant at about 1,2 million.

Many well-known international dairy and beef-cattle breeds, as well as various important indigenous breeds, such as the Afrikaner, Drakensberger, Bonsmara and Nguni are found in South Africa. These breeds are systematically and scientifically improved with the aid of performance testing and visual appraisal based on functional efficiency to increase production and reproduction. Due to the relatively low carrying capacity of natural pasturage (83 million ha), cattle-ranching is extensive in the lower rainfall regions.

The wool clip is the fourth largest in the world (92 000 tons). The main breeds of sheep are fine-wooled Merino (59%), the South African mutton Merino, Dohne-Merino, Dormer, Dorper (the last-mentioned two are locally developed breeds) and the Karakul, of which the pelts are marketed worldwide. The main sheep-farming area is the Karoo. The Karakul industry is limited to the dry northwestern regions of the Cape Province. The mohair industry yields 40 to 45% of world production. Angoras constitute 74% of all goats in South Africa. The remainder are Boer goats bred for meat production.

The Marketing Act of 1937 (superseded by the consolidated Marketing Act of 1968) introduced marketing programmes for most agricultural products. Administered by control boards, the programmes are designed to promote stability in production and prices, and orderly distribution and marketing.

It is partly due to the research and extensive work undertaken in many fields over a period of several decades that South Africa's farmers manage to feed a growing population in adverse agricultural conditions. The Department of Agricultural Development main-

A blue gum plantation in the Eastern Transvaal
(Photograph: T F J van Rensburg)

tains specialist research institutes for citrus and sub-tropical fruit, tobacco and cotton, vegetables and or-namental plants, fruit and fruit technology, viticulture and oenology, animal and dairy science, grain crops, soil and irrigation, and plant protection and research centres for grassland and plant biotechnology. The Veterinary Research Institute at Onderstepoort re-searches animal diseases and public health risks arising from animal products. It is also responsible for produc-ing many types of vaccines against animal diseases. Approximately 154 million doses of vaccine against 58 different diseases were sold in 1990/91. Many of these diseases are endemic to Africa and the prophylactics, some of which are not manufactured elsewhere, play a crucial role in the fight against economically ravaging diseases in many regions of the continent.

Farmers' main source of finance is the Land and Agricultural Bank, established in 1912. Today the Bank grants long, medium and short-term loans to farmers, agricultural co-operatives, control boards and statutory institutions.

Forestry
South Africa is virtually self-sufficient in its require-ments for timber and wood products. Imports are specialised timber products such as hardwood, furni-ture wood and certain types of wood for high-quality paper. The book value of the timber industry (planta-tions and mills) exceeds R 16 000 million.

Forests cover 1,36 million ha (just over 1% of the country's total surface area). They comprise exotic commercial plantations (1 200 000 ha) and indigenous high forests (164 000 ha). Natural forests comprise high forests, scrub forests and savannah. High forests are found mainly in the mountains along the coastal strip from Cape Town eastwards, and northwards to the Soutpansberg Range in the Northern Transvaal. The largest continuous area is a strip, 180 km long and 16 km wide, from George through Knysna to Humansdorp in the Southern Cape Province. The species include yellowwood, stinkwood, white pear, black ironwood, assegai and kamassi. Since 1968 about 2 000 m³ of round logs have been felled and sold annually according to guidelines contained in a scientific conservation programme. The prices realised for prime stinkwood logs at auctions make this wood one of the world's most expensive furniture timbers. Scrub and savannah forests cover extensive areas in the drier parts of the Transvaal and Natal.

About half of the exotic plantation area is planted with pines and other softwoods, about 40% to eucalypts (mainly *Eucalyptus grandis*) and about 10% to wattle (mostly in Natal). The plantations are distributed as follows: Transvaal and Orange Free State 50%, Natal 39%, and the Cape Province 11%. Pines and eucalypts mature much more rapidly in South Africa than in the northern hemisphere. Trees can be felled after eight years for use as mine props and small poles, after 10 years for wattle bark and chips, after 15 to 20 years for pulpwood and after 25 years for sawn timber. The plantations produce more than 16,5 million m³ of roundwood logs which are processed into sawn or planed timber, treated wooden poles, wood-based panel products, mining timber, woodpulp, paper and paperboard, and other miscellaneous products. There are more than 240 timber-processing factories and plants in South Africa.

Foresters are trained at the Saasveld Forestry School near George, and the University of Stellenbosch offers the only degree course in forestry.

Fisheries

More than 500 000 tons of fish (marine mammals excluded) were caught and landed in 1990, more than 90% from the cold waters of the Atlantic Ocean along the West Coast. The wholesale value of the industry's total output was about R1 180 million in 1990. The fishing fleet consists of approximately 4 500 vessels of various

Clams, black mussels and oysters are cultivated at a seafarm in Saldanha Bay

sizes and about 27 500 people are employed in the fishing industry and related activities.

The principal species of shoal fish caught by inshore coastal trawlers are anchovy (58% of a total of 259 000 tons), pilchard (22%) and round herring (17%). These are processed into meal, oil and canned products. The most important varieties brought in by deep-sea trawlers are Cape hake (57%), kingklip (rock-cod, 1,8%), snoek (sea-pike, 5,2%), horse mackerel (18,6%), monkfish (2,3%), club mackerel (6%), sole (0,4%) and squid (0,3%). The most important species caught by handline are tuna, cod, snoek, silverfish, geelbek (Cape salmon) and yellowtail. Cape rock lobster is harvested along the West Coast and other varieties along the East and South coasts. About 80% of the total catch is exported. Catches or harvests of less significance include abalone, pink prawns, langoustines, mullet, oysters, redbait and octopus. Exotic species of oysters are also cultivated. Substantial quantities of sea-weed are collected as well as guano from offshore islands.

A fishing zone of 200 nautical miles has been enforced along the coastline since 1977, to prevent over-exploitation by foreign fleets. The Government also applies a strict conservation policy, including closed seasons, factory quotas, and limits on factories and vessels to protect South Africa's fish resources.

Research on South Africa's fish resources is done by the Research Institute of the Department of Sea Fisheries and is divided into environmental studies, inshore resources and offshore resources. The work consists of studies done on environmental pollution, biological oceanography, the monitoring of sea life which entails stock assessment, commercial catch statistics, biological characteristics, seals and sea-birds.

WATER

South Africa is a dry country. (See *Geography* and *Agriculture, Forestry and Fisheries*.) The combined average annual flow of the rivers is about 53 000 million cubic metres (m^3). However, much of this volume is lost through flood spillage and evaporation, so that each year only about 33 000 million m^3 can be economically utilised.

In addition, underground water-supplies annually yield about 5 400 million m^3. At the same time the annual demand for water by agriculture, industries and urban areas grows by about 1,6%. Should this trend continue, the total demand for water will be about 22 500 million m^3 a year by the year 2000, or only 15 900 million m^3 less than the maximum available at present from storage dams and underground sources.

The Cahora Bassa project in Mozambique, a joint venture with South Africa, shows how Africa's natural resources can be harnessed to benefit the whole subcontinent

Hence the fact that engineers of South Africa's water authorities, particularly the Department of Water Affairs and Forestry, are urgently investigating ways and means of increasing water-supplies so that general economic development will not be impeded by shortages. The investigations cover three main areas — better methods of developing and utilising existing resources, more efficient use of developed supplies, and new sources such as the desalination of sea-water.

Currently more than 300 South African dams are included in the world register of large dams. With the current level of technology and expertise, the total annual storage capacity of all dams in South Africa is approximately 33 000 million m^3. A number of large storage and interbasin transfer projects have been initiated by the Department of Water Affairs and Forestry to ensure an adequate water-supply to all water users in South Africa:

— The largest water development project ever undertaken in South Africa — the **Orange River Project** — is aimed at making maximum use of the 7 500 million m^3 of water which annually flows down the country's largest river into the Atlantic Ocean. About 300 000 ha could potentially be irrigated and 2 200 million m^3 of water be made available annually for urban and industrial consumption. The project comprises the Hendrik Verwoerd Dam, the P K le Roux Dam, the Van der Kloof Canal System and the Orange-Fish River Tunnel. The tunnel diverts water from the Hendrik Verwoerd Dam to the Great Fish River Valley in the Eastern Cape where the Lower Fish River State Water Project, a joint venture with Ciskei, is being built. It also diverts water to the Fish-Sundays Canal System, which includes the 13,1 km Cookhouse Tunnel; the De Mistkraal Weir, which was completed in 1987 and increased the flow to the Sundays River to 22 m^3 per second, thus practically doubling irrigation in the Sundays River Valley; and the Lower Sundays River State Water Scheme.

— The **Vaal River System**, including the Komati and Usutu rivers, can yield 3 000 million m^3 annually, supplying water to the most economically important regions in South Africa. These are the industries of the Pretoria/Witwatersrand/Vereeniging (PWV) area, the Eastern Transvaal highveld coalfields, the goldfields of the Southwestern Transvaal and the Orange Free State, and many irrigation projects — including the one at Vaalharts, the biggest irrigation project in South Africa.

The system comprises the Grootdraai, Vaal and Bloemhof dams. The Tugela-Vaal Scheme is a combined water-transfer and pumped-storage project undertaken jointly by the national electricity utility company, Eskom (see *Energy*), and the Department of Water Affairs and Forestry. Each year 550 million m^3 of water is transferred to the Vaal River basin and 1 000 megawatt (Mw) is produced during peak periods.

— Large-scale development on the Eastern Transvaal highveld necessitated various water-transfer projects to ensure an adequate water-supply to this region. The **Usutu River Scheme** was designed to supply water to the Camden, Kriel, Kendal and Matla thermal power stations of Eskom which are situated on the highveld in the Vaal River Catchment Area. The scheme consists of the Jericho, Westoe and Morgenstond dams in the Usutu River Catchment Area from where water is pumped to these four power stations.

The Usutu-Vaal River Scheme comprises the Grootdraai Dam. The supply from the Grootdraai Dam is augmented with water from the Heyshope Dam on the Assegai River, a tributary of the Great Usutu River.

The Komati-Usutu River Scheme, consisting of the Vygeboom and Nooitgedacht dams, supplies the Arnot, Hendrina, Komati and Duvha power stations and is linked to the Usutu-Vaal River Scheme at the Witbank Dam.

Ultimately the entire system is linked to form a network by means of which, should any of these projects fail to supply enough water to its users, water can be transferred from one project to another to augment the supply.

— The **Riviersonderend-Berg River Project** is part of projects in the Western Cape that are designed to develop the potential of the Riviersonderend, Elands, Eerste and Berg rivers in the region. The various components of the project are: the Theewaterskloof Dam, the 23 km Jonkershoek Tunnel System which, together with two diversion weirs and two dams, will provide surplus water for urban, industrial and irrigation purposes, and an intricate water distribution system, still to be constructed, in the Berg and Eerste river valleys which will provide water for irrigation.

— The **Palmiet River Scheme** is the second dual-purpose water project in South Africa (Tugela-Vaal being the first). The first phase comprises a combined hydro-electric pumped-storage and water-supply system that adds about 400 Mw to the national grid of Eskom and augments the water-supply to the Cape metropolitan area by about 30 million m^3 annually. The project consists of the Kogelberg and Rockview dams, which are linked by a tunnel of two kilometres, and the hydro-electric power station at Kogelberg Dam. From the Rockview Dam a 3,35 km conduit conveys the water intended for Cape Town to the Steenbras Dam, which supplies that metropolitan area with water. A possible further phase of development of the Palmiet River is at present being considered in accordance with the guidelines for Integrated Environmental Management which incorporates a public involvement programme.

— The **Knellpoort Dam** was completed in 1988 to augment the supply of water from the Rustfontein Dam on the Modder River to the Bloemfontein area, by means of the inter-basin transfer of water. This transfer takes place from the nearby Welbedacht Dam on the Caledon River via the Knellpoort Dam to the headwaters of the Modder River in the vicinity of Dewetsdorp.

The Knellpoort Dam, the first rollcrete-arch gravity dam in the world, is also intended to counteract the problem caused by the silting up of the Welbedacht Dam on the Caledon River. The high rate of sedimentation has reduced the gross capacity of the Welbedacht Dam within 16 years, from its original 115 million m^3 to about 30 million m^3 at present.

— In 1986 an agreement was signed between the governments of Lesotho and South Africa for the construction of the **Lesotho Highlands Water Project**. This project will provide a major boost to Lesotho's economy. It is being developed in four phases in accordance with water demand projections for South Africa. Eventually Lesotho will generate approximately 1 260 Gigawatt of hydro-electricity hourly per year to meet the country's internal demand while at the same time delivering $70 m^3$ of water per second to South Africa. When fully developed, the project will consist of five major dams ranging from 126 m to 180 m in height with a total active storage capacity of 6,5 km^3; two power stations with a total installed capacity of 110 Mw; a smaller dam, 55 m high, forming the tailpond of the hydro-electric power station; a total of 225 km of tunnels; three pumping stations, and new and upgraded access roads totalling 650 km.

This project is a major element in the growing trend towards economic cooperation between South Africa and its neighbours in the region, and is co-financed by the World Bank, the European Community (EC) and similar international organisations.

The Malibamats'o Bridge, which towers 80 m above the river-bed, was completed in 1990 and is immediately downstream of the future transfer-tunnel intake. The contract for the construction of the Katse Dam was awarded to a consortium of contractors consisting of companies from the following countries: France, Germany, Italy, the Republic of South Africa and the United Kingdom. The contract for the construction of the Delivery Tunnel North was awarded to a joint venture between Germany, South Africa and Switzerland.

ENERGY

By the early 1980s South Africa had become a net exporter of energy and was rapidly achieving a high level of energy self-sufficiency. At the end of the decade South Africa was facing a rising demand for energy that could double by the beginning of the next century.

Coal provides about 83% of the country's primary energy needs. At present, in situ mineable coal reserves are estimated at 115 530 million tons of which 55 000 million tons (58,4 billion tons in 1982) can be extracted economically by means of current technology and mining methods.

Approximately 147 000 GWh (Gigawatt hour) of electricity was sent out in South Africa in 1990. Of this, the national electricity utility company, Eskom, accounted for almost 93% — at an average price of 7,88 cents per kw/h. Eskom runs a national grid of more than 220 000 km of high-voltage transmission lines to supply electricity throughout the country. Electricity is also exported to the self-governing territories and some neighbouring countries. Eskom operated 18 coal-fired power stations which consumed 70,8 million tons of coal during 1990. The total installed capacity amounted to more than 35 673 megawatt (Mw) during 1990. Because the flow of South Africa's rivers is generally seasonal, hydro-electricity can be generated only at large storage dams such as the Hendrik Verwoerd (320 Mw) and P K le Roux (220 Mw) dams on the Orange River. The Drakensberg pumped-storage project (see *Water*) can generate 1 000 Mw of hydro-electricity in peak periods. Hydro-electricity presents an alternative source of energy once the vast hydro-resources of Southern Africa are harnessed.

South Africa's first nuclear power station, at Koeberg north of Cape Town, which has a generating capacity of 1 930 Mw, came on stream in 1984/85. The country has 13,6% of the Western World's uranium resources and is one of the world's three largest producers of uranium.

Initially, enriched uranium fuel elements for Koeberg were imported. However, the enrichment plant of the Atomic Energy Corporation (AEC) at Valindaba, near

In the electricity research laboratory of the CSIR, Pretoria, high voltage testing of insulation is carried out

Pretoria, is geared to produce sufficient material for the country's nuclear fuel requirements. The AEC also has a wide-ranging capability in related products, technology and services. Over the years it has built up a significant capability in the production, supply and application of medical and industrial isotopes.

The future of uranium enrichment in South Africa will naturally be closely associated with the nuclear energy programme of Eskom, which is aimed at guaranteed supply and the most economical enrichment. South Africa's uranium and thorium will be the primary future energy resource once coal reserves become depleted. South Africa is a signatory to the Nuclear Non-proliferation Treaty.

Coal is also the base of the growing South African synfuel industry. Sasol 1 in the Orange Free State produced its first petroleum products from coal in 1955. The international oil crisis of 1973 prompted the construction of Sasol 2 at a cost of R2 500 million and Sasol 3 at R3 276 million. Both plants are located at Secunda in the Eastern Transvaal coalfields. Sasol 2 reached full production in 1982 and Sasol 3 in 1985. For decades these were the only commercially viable oil-from-coal plants in operation anywhere in the world. They will eventually produce a substantial proportion of South Africa's liquid fuel requirements, as well as a host of other products usually derived from the refining of imported crude oil. Fuel gas for industrial purposes is also produced in large quantities.

The search for oil continues on the continental shelf round the country. So far there has been no economically viable oil strike. However, several important gas finds have been made, notably one south of Mossel Bay with a potential yield exceeding four million m^3 daily for 30 years. A natural gas conversion plant at Mossel Bay for producing synthetic fuels is under construction and is expected to come into operation in 1992.

The National Energy Council (NEC) was created in November 1987 in accordance with the Energy Act of 1987. It also represents the interests of consumers, distributors and producers. The aims of the Energy Act are paraphrased in the charter of the NEC: namely to direct, promote and coordinate South Africa's energy interests in co-operation with the private and public sectors.

MINING

South Africa, one of the major mineral-producing countries of the world and the main exporter of minerals, has the largest known reserves of gold, chromium, platinum, vanadium, manganese and andalusite. Moreover, it has substantial deposits of many other minerals, principally coal, uranium, diamonds, iron, zirconium, titanium, fluorspar, nickel and phosphates.

About 80% of the South African mineral production is exported to various industrialised countries, mainly in Western Europe, North America and the Far East. The 1990 export sales value amounted to R 29 699 million, representing about 49% of the total foreign revenue. Domestic sales were worth an additional R 8 348 million. In monetary terms, gold is South Africa's single most important export commodity.

Gold and uranium

With a current annual output of about 600 tons of gold, South Africa is the major producer of this metal in the world. The value of gold production, in current terms, first exceeded 10 digits in 1980, when world prices reached record levels. It totalled approximately R 19 000 million in 1990.

The production of uranium, essentially a by-product of gold mining, peaked in 1983, after which it declined due to weakening demand worldwide. In 1990, South Africa ranked seventh among producers of uranium oxide in the West. About 85% of South Africa's output in 1990 was obtained from four goldmines, 11% reclaimed from goldmine residues and 4% as a by-product of copper mining.

Diamonds

South Africa is a major producer of natural diamonds (and gem diamonds in particular) which occur mainly in kimberlite 'pipes' at Kimberley and Postmasburg, and near Pretoria. Stones are also recovered from alluvial fields in Namaqualand and the seabed off the West Coast. Production totalled 8,7 million carats in 1990.

Platinum

The platinum-group metals — platinum, palladium, rhodium, ruthenium, iridium and osmium — occur within the confines of the Bushveld Igneous Complex, one of the largest metal-bearing geological entities in the world. Reserves of these metals are sufficient to last for many generations. An important use of platinum and rhodium is as catalysts in equipment that detoxifies exhaust fumes from automobiles.

The Groot Geluk coppermine at Ellisras in the North-western Transvaal

Chromium

More than 74% of the world's reserve of chromium ore is contained in the Bushveld Igneous Complex. South Africa is well established as the major supplier of this commodity in the West. The foremost application of the metal lies in the manufacture of stainless steel, but it is also extensively used in the chemical and refractory industries.

Manganese

This metal, essential for steel production, is derived from ore mined in the Northwestern Cape, where about 80% of world reserves are found. South Africa is the main producer of both manganese ore and manganese alloys. In 1990 sales of manganese ore were valued at R848 million. Approximately 4,4 million tons of manganese ore, of which 2,2 million tons were exported, were produced in 1990.

Coal

South Africa's in situ mineable coal reserves are estimated at 115 530 million tons, of which 55 000 million tons can be recovered. Coal is the country's most important fuel for generating electricity and is the primary raw material for conversion into liquid synthetic petroleum products. Production of saleable coal by some 110 mines totals more than 175 million tons annually and could rise to about 210 million tons by the year 2000. Between 1985 and 1991 several new large coalmines commenced production. The value of the total annual production currently exceeds R8 000 million, and was second only to gold in 1990.

Other minerals

Other South African minerals which have world significance include copper, silver, tin, antimony, zinc and lead. South Africa also produces andalusite, asbestos, feldspar, fluorspar, granite, gypsum, limestone, magnesite, mica, marble, phosphate rock, tiger-eye, salt, silica and special clays, vermiculite and wonderstone.

All told more than 60 minerals are mined in South Africa by an industry employing approximately 700 000 workers.

Mineral processing

This industry has progressed to such an extent that South Africa is the largest beneficiator and supplier of ferroalloys, vanadium pentoxide and manganese metal in the world. In addition, South Africa is an important beneficiator and exporter of silicon metal, phosphoric acid, titanium and vanadium slag, and antimony trioxide.

INDUSTRY

Manufacturing accounts for more than a fifth — the largest single share — of South Africa's gross domestic product (GDP).

In recent years the industrial base has been widened to such an extent that South Africa can manufacture most of its essential imports should it be necessary. The main stimuli for industrial development have been an abundance of natural resources (see *Mining* and *Agriculture, Forestry and Fisheries*), well-developed communications and transport networks, government incentives, a strong entrepreneurial reservoir with the necessary know-how, a growing market and a vast labour pool.

The underlying strength of the economy is further reinforced by rapid urbanisation, which again stimulates industrial development in many spheres.

Processed foodstuffs
Generally, 40% of total production is consumed locally and the balance exported. Important components of this sector include the dairy, baking and sugar industries, processing of meat and canning of fish.

Textiles and clothing
The most important products are knitted goods and blankets, and industries such as spinning and weaving.

Chemicals
This sector is divided into the following main components:

Basic industrial chemicals
This component includes products such as fertilisers, pesticides, insecticides, fungicides, plastic raw materials, man-made fibres, synthetic rubber, explosives,

ammonia, pitch, alcohols, paraffin waxes, liquid gases, nitrogen, sulphuric acid, superphosphates, cyanide and other acids, oil and various petroleum products from coal, alcohols, paraffin waxes, caustic soda, hydrogen chloride, hydrochloric acid, and phosphate concentrates as a raw material for fertiliser manufacturers. A wide range of plastics and other products are made from coal. South Africa leads the world in coal-based manufacture and expertise. Several chemical plants manufacture vast quantities of PVC and other plastics, resins, phosphoric acid, as well as chemical materials for atomic fission and fusion, and a host of other basic industrial chemicals. A further important addition is the manufacture of petroleum from natural gas along the South Coast of South Africa.

Other chemicals
This component includes the manufacture of paints, varnishes, stains, shellac, lacquers, enamels and japans.

Pharmaceuticals
A wide variety of drugs and medicines is produced. These include vaccines, serums, plasmas, antibiotics, quinine, sulpha drugs, pharmaceutical preparations for human and veterinary use, soaps, cleaning materials, perfumes, cosmetics and toilet preparations.

Metal industries
Base metals
The Government established Iscor in 1928 to promote the development of the iron and steel industry and allied industries. In 1989 Iscor was privatised as part of the Government's privatisation policy. At present Iscor has three plants — Pretoria, Vanderbijlpark and Newcastle. Other manufacturers produce a wide range of special steels such as abrasion-resistant steel, carbon and stainless steels, as well as copper, brass, ferroalloys and high-carbon chrome (see *Mining*). The country's largest engineering works manufactures parts for

The blast furnace complex of the Vanderbijlpark Works of Iscor

cranes and crane machinery, turbine casings, boiler drums, sugar mills and other heavy equipment. Large quantities of aluminium are also produced annually.

Metal products
These include structural steel, sheet metal products, cables, wire products, pipes and fittings, tin ware and roller bearings.

Machinery
This sector includes the production of engines, turbines, agricultural machinery and implements, machine tools, special industrial machinery, and office computing and accounting machines. South Africa makes most of the agricultural implements it requires and also exports a considerable proportion of these products.

Transport equipment
South Africa has a well-developed motor vehicle industry capable of manufacturing a full range of vehicles

from light cars to heavy off-road and underground mining vehicles. Today 19 vehicle manufacturers are active in the market. They are supported by a large and diversified components industry. Apart from supplying the local market, exports of vehicles and components are rising steadily. The local manufacture and export of passenger cars, commercial vehicles and buses as well as automotive components for these vehicles are encouraged through a phased local-content programme.

A well-developed industry which manufactures and exports all types of railroad equipment exists in South Africa. The industry also supplies and maintains the extensive rail network in Southern Africa. Extensive shipbuilding and repair facilities exist at the country's major ports.

Non-metallic mineral products
This section comprises the manufacture of bricks, tiles, pipes, crucibles, cement, cement-asbestos products, oven linings and refractories.

Decentralisation
South Africa, in conjunction with Transkei, Bophuthatswana, Venda and Ciskei, has an active programme of regional industrial development. In terms of this programme, financial incentives are offered for the establishment and expansion of manufacturing industries at identified development points, thereby distributing industrial development more evenly throughout the country.

Through the years industrial development has been concentrated in four metropolitan areas, while little industrial development took place in the rural parts. The regional development programme for industries is the main component of the Government's steps to implement a regional development strategy.

The main aims of this programme are to:
— better spatial distribution of economic activity with a view to preventing metropolitan overconcentration

and to stimulate industrial development in a regional context
— distribute income more evenly by providing additional employment opportunities where these are needed most
— better utilisation of the available infrastructure and development potential of the various regions and points.

The present incentives introduced in April 1982 consist of an attractive package of concessions on employment and investment, as well as transport rebates, housing subsidies and a tender price preference. These incentives have proved popular and over the first eight years in South Africa alone, more than 4 400 new projects have been established involving an investment of more than R5 056 million.

The programme is making a significant impact on industrial and related development as well as on employment in the rural areas.

South African Bureau of Standards (SABS)
The SABS, established in 1945 to promote quality and standardisation in the South African manufacturing industry, has 60 laboratories where virtually every product made in South Africa can be tested.

CSIR
Since the CSIR was founded in 1945, it has provided valuable research and development support for South African industry. The CSIR's research, development and implementation activities centre in 14 operational divisions. The CSIR derives a substantial proportion of its income from contract work carried out for private industry and government agencies.

Foundation for Research Development
The Foundation for Research Development (FRD) is an independent science foundation which has the vital

task of promoting the development of human resources in the field of science and technology. Special emphasis is placed on enabling disadvantaged communities to make their full contribution to science and technology by providing them with the relevant expertise and innovative skills in those fields which satisfy local market needs.

The FRD Schools Programme and University Development Programme focus on the institutions where the majority of black students undergo secondary and tertiary education. At universities, FRD grants are made to staff and students to support further study and research, as well as to promote national and international contact. Outreach actions to schools include enrichment of teachers and the development of educational technologies and resources to promote science and mathematics tuition. Needs at the different institutions are identified and prioritised. Actions to address these needs are developed through a process of formal and informal discussions with staff, students, and other delegates from various educational and private organisations.

INDUSTRIAL RELATIONS

Labour policy is based on the following principles:
— There should be minimum interference by the Government in the employer-employee relationship
— Order, stability and security must be maintained in the labour field
— Consultation must take place between the State, employers and employees
— No discrimination based on race or colour.

The structural elements of industrial relations are often referred to as 'freedoms' or basic human 'rights'. These are entrenched in labour legislation and consist of the following:
— the right to work
— the right to associate
— the right to collective bargaining
— the right to withhold labour
— the right to protection
— the right to development
— the right to security against unemployment and injury on duty
— the right to job security and protection against unfair labour practices.

The labour field and especially labour relations is a highly dynamic and sensitive facet of modern society. This is even more pronounced in a developing country such as South Africa, particularly since the composition of the players is so unique and complex. The Government is acutely aware of the importance of all labour-related issues and for this reason the National Manpower Commission was established in 1979. In terms of the Labour Relations Act, the Commission's functions are to
— advise the Minister either on its own initiative or as directed
— conduct and promote continuous research across the entire manpower field
— seek close liaison on manpower matters with other

government departments and institutions, the private
sector, educational institutions, and trade unions
— report annually and on an ad hoc basis.

Negotiation/dispute-settling mechanisms
Labour legislation
In order to promote sound labour relations in South
Africa guidelines and instructions are contained in the
Labour Relations Act of 1956, the Wage Act of 1957
and the Basic Conditions of Employment Act of 1983,
in addition to statutory bodies such as the Industrial
Court and the Labour Appeal Court.
The Labour Relations Act of 1956: The objects of the

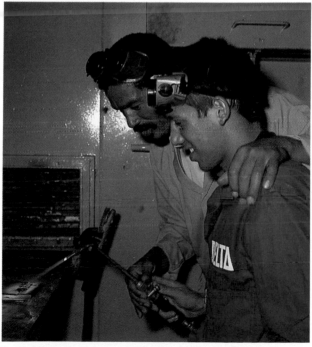

*In order to promote good labour relations, employers pro-
vide a happy environment for their employees*

Labour Relations Act are the registration and orderly administration of trade unions, employers' organisations and industrial councils; the prevention and settlement of disputes between employers and employees, and the regulation of conditions of employment by way of arbitration, mediation, agreements and orders. The Act does not apply to all sectors of the economically active population of South Africa. Notable exceptions are employees from the State and the agricultural sectors. The Government will, during the 1991/1992 parliamentary sessions, consider extending the scope of application of certain labour legislation to include agricultural workers.

Industrial Court: The Industrial Court has the task of maintaining industrial peace. Permanent courts have been established in Pretoria, Durban, Johannesburg and Cape Town, with Pretoria as the official statutory seat. The Court also regularly hears cases in other centres.

Labour Appeal Court: With effect from 1 September 1988 a Labour Appeal Court consisting of six separate divisions (corresponding to the areas of jurisdiction and seats of the divisions of the Supreme Court) was established in terms of section 17(A) of the Labour Relations Act of 1956. In terms of the Act this court is empowered to

— decide any question of law arising from proceedings in the Industrial Court
— decide appeals against decisions of the Industrial Court relating to the determination of unfair labour practices or any order as to costs
— review proceedings of the Industrial Court.

Wage Act of 1957: The objects of the Wage Act are the establishment of the Wage Board, and the determination of minimum wages and other conditions of employment for employees who are not organised or not sufficiently organised to make effective use of the negotiation mechanisms of the Labour Relations Act.

Basic Conditions of Employment Act of 1983: The purpose of the Act is to ensure basic conditions of employment for all workers in the private and local government sectors (excluding farm labourers, employees in private households and employees of the State) who are not subject to the relevant provisions of the Labour Relations Act of 1956, the Mines and Works Act of 1956, the Wage Act of 1957 and the Manpower Training Act of 1981.

Industrial councils: Industrial councils are, in terms of South African legislation, autonomous bodies consisting of equal employer and employee representation. Only registered employers' organisations and trade unions may become parties to an industrial council. Industrial councils endeavour to prevent labour disputes between employers and employees and to settle disputes which arise. This function is mainly performed by the negotiation of collective labour agreements.

Activities of industrial councils, 1986-1990

Year	Disputes settled
1986	697
1987	839
1988	1 319
1989	1 503
1990	1 108

Conciliation boards: A conciliation board is an ad hoc body established to try to resolve a dispute where there is no industrial council that has jurisdiction to settle the matter. Such a board consists of an equal number of representatives of the employers and employees concerned.

In total, 8 461 applications for the establishment of conciliation boards were received during the period 1 November 1989 to 31 October 1990. In 6 142 of these cases, conciliation boards were established while in 2 185 cases, the applications did not comply with the prescribed legal requirements and boards could not be established; 46 applications were withdrawn and 88 are receiving attention. Of the 6 142 applications that were approved, the conciliation boards succeeded in settling 989 disputes while 3 020 reached deadlock during negotiations and 999 applications were withdrawn after the conciliation boards had already been established. At the end of October 1990, 1 134 conciliation boards were still engaged in negotiations.

Trade unions
The granting of trade union rights to all workers including the removal of all discriminatory legislation from the country's labour and industrial systems nearly a decade ago, not only brought about a sharp rise in trade union membership, but also in trade union activities.

The upward trend in union membership is still continuing. At the end of 1990, nearly three million employees belonged to trade unions constituting about 25% of the total economically active population. According to available records the number of strikes and mandays lost since 1986 were:

Year	Strikes	Mandays lost
1986	798	1 308 958
1987	1 148	5 825 231
1988	1 025	914 388
1989	855	1 238 686
1990	848	2 973 921

The relatively high number of mandays lost during 1987 was mainly due to a dispute in the mining sector resulting in a strike lasting approximately three weeks.

The average duration of strikes is regarded as still relatively low and the statistics for the corresponding period are:

Year	Days
1986	3,1
1987	9,9
1988	5,6
1989	7,0
1990	8,5

A number of trade union federations have been formed. The most significant being the Congress of South African Trade Unions (Cosatu) with 14 affiliates and a predominantly black membership of more than one million. The largest of its affiliates is the National Union of Metalworkers of South Africa and the National

Union of Mine Workers (Numsa). Both have in excess of 250 000 members.

In terms of labour legislation, registration of trade unions at the Department of Manpower is voluntary and the number of registered trade unions since 1986 varied between 195 in 1986 and 209 in 1990.

Manpower Training Act

The Act provides the foundation for the development and improvement of skills.

The essential characteristics of this Act are:
— its placement of responsibility for training on the shoulders of employers and employee organisations
— its non-discriminatory tone, providing for the training of all workers
— its all-embracing character, providing for the training of all categories of workers.

Parliament amended the Act in April 1990 in order to achieve these objectives and to keep pace with changing circumstances in the economy and industry, as well as to present government policy of entrusting the training of employees to the private sector. The Amendment Act paved the way for a new training system, namely the establishment and accreditation of training boards, whereby industry accepts the responsibility for the structuring and control of apprentice training and other training.

The Act provides for the establishment of a revolving fund for the training of unemployed people. The purpose of the fund is to draw contributions from the private sector which are, together with funds voted by Parliament, used to finance training whereby unemployed people are equipped with working skills that facilitate their entry into the labour market. Although the scheme initially emphasised the needs of the unemployed and simultaneously addressed some of the present-day socio-economic problems, it assisted in alleviating the shortage of skilled manpower, albeit at lower levels.

Of the almost 1,4 million people trained since 1985,

approximately 25% were placed in the formal sector immediately after their training or were able to find a livelihood in the informal sector of the economy. Because of the growing awareness of informal-sector activities in South Africa, it is assumed that entrepreneurial-skills training will become an optional part of basic training.

Unemployment Insurance Act
The main purpose of the Unemployment Insurance Fund is to insure contributors to a certain extent and for a specified period against loss of earnings, and to provide for lump sum payments to the dependants of deceased contributors. Loss of earnings can arise from unemployment, due to termination of employment, illness, maternity leave or the adoption of children.

Workmen's Compensation Act
This Act provides the framework for the existence of the Workmen's Compensation Fund, to which only employers contribute in terms of an annual assessment made by the Workmen's Compensation Commissioner. The Fund compensates all workmen for work-related injuries. Compensation includes medical expenses, wages lost during a period of temporary disablement (75% of such wages with a maximum determined by the Act), lump sums or pensions for partial or total disablement, pensions for dependants in the event of death and burial expenses.

Guidance and Placement Act
This Act provides for the counselling and placement of all workseekers and potential employees and is aimed at the optimal realisation of potential. It also regulates the registration of private employment offices.

Machinery and Occupational Safety Act
The Act provides for the safety of employees at their place of employment, or in the course of their duty, or when working with machinery.

The Advisory Council for Occupational Safety was established in terms of section 4 of the Act. It is the policy of the Government that in drafting safety legislation, all three parties, namely the State, the employer and the employee, be involved jointly. All three parties are represented on the Advisory Council.

The Act and its allied regulations are administrated by expert inspectors who are appointed by the Minister. The inspectors do basic or preventative inspections, inspection of building and construction work, and elevator, escalator and boiler inspections. Inspectors also control the handling, processing and use of materials which might be potential health hazards, to ensure that the safety criteria are met.

Incidents in which persons at work or users of machinery are killed or seriously injured, must be reported to and investigated by an inspector. The results of such investigations are sent to the various Attorneys-General and are statistically processed by the Department. Inspectors are also concerned with administrative and legal work, training, interviews and visits to employers.

FOREIGN TRADE

Trade with other countries is very important to the South African economy, so much so that the country is ranked among the 25 most active Western trading nations.

South Africa trades both in Africa and the rest of the world. The products traded in, cover virtually every product category from raw and beneficiated materials and agricultural products to industrial commodities and capital goods.

The country's trade relations are regulated multilaterally by the General Agreement on Tariffs and Trade (Gatt). In the event of trade problems arising, such issues are normally resolved bilaterally between the governments concerned. Only if a solution cannot be found, is the matter referred to Gatt for further attention and arbitration.

South Africa is categorised as a developing country by the International Monetary Fund and as a developed

In 1991 South Africa exhibited at the Kenya International Show where the Premier Group of companies received the prize for the best international stand

country by Gatt. The goal of economic policy in South Africa is to expand the scope and extent of the industrial base. This is viewed as crucial to South Africa's economic growth, particularly in the light of its rapidly expanding population. The country continually endeavours to develop new products for both the domestic and overseas markets and is in fact a net importer of capital equipment for use in its manufacturing sector.

While imports into South Africa originate from round the globe the country has, after many years' experience become known as a reliable supplier of a vast range of products to countries the world over.

In the past, South Africa exported much of the raw minerals, metals and ores that abound in the country. This practice is at present being re-evaluated with a view to beneficiating them locally, thereby increasing their value. These primary products are of great importance to and in demand for overseas industrial technologies and production processes.

South Africa's export trade is promoted by the Department of Trade and Industry, which has a Chief Directorate and four directorates specialising in all matters related to trade promotion. Through the Chief Directorate and its present network of representatives in 38 cities worldwide, assistance is given to exporters in the form of export incentives and a wide range of gratis trade services.

Since significant improvement has come about in South Africa's trade relations with African states and Central and East European countries, numerous permanent trade representatives have been appointed in these countries. Trade agreements have been signed with Madagascar, Poland, Romania and Hungary, while various others are in advanced stages of negotiation. On 15 December 1990 the European Community (EC) lifted the ban on new investments in South Africa. Sanctions are gradually being relaxed, allowing South Africa gradually to resume its rightful role in international trade and in the development of Africa. In October 1991 Japan lifted trade and financial sanctions against South

Africa. This step immediately triggered an estimated R 1 billion iron ore export contract with steel producers in Japan.

Private-sector bodies, such as the South African Foreign Trade Organisation (Safto), also actively assist exporters with useful advice on managing and developing foreign markets.

Useful addresses
South African Foreign Trade Organisation (Safto)
PO Box 782706
Sandton
2146
Republic of South Africa
Tel: (011) 883-3737

Department of Trade and Industry
Private Bag X84
Pretoria
0001
Republic of South Africa
Tel: (012) 310-9791

TRANSPORT

South Africa's modern and extensive transport system plays an important role in oiling the wheels of the national economy and also those of other African states. A number of countries in Southern Africa move their imports and exports to and from the region with the aid of the South African transport infrastructure.

Roads

The quality of a country's road network is a good measure of its economic welfare. South Africa's complete road network links settlements ranging from the largest metropolitan area to the smallest village and comprises a total length of more than 206 000 km. Of this network more than 57 000 km are surfaced. It has been estimated that the road network represents a capital investment of R 82 000 million in current money terms.

Roads are provided and maintained by all three tiers of government — the central government (Department of Transport, South African Roads Board), provincial councils and local authorities (city or town councils). Overall transport plans have been compiled for eight metropolitan transport areas, of which the core cities are Johannesburg, Cape Town, Pretoria, Durban, Port Elizabeth, Springs, Bloemfontein and Pietermaritzburg.

Direct taxes generally finance national and provincial highways and roads. In 1983 the Department of Transport decided to introduce a toll system as an additional source of revenue for road construction. Major freeways have been upgraded and or constructed to function as toll roads. Expenditure on national roads amounted to R 674 million in 1990/91.

In 1990 South Africa had about six million registered vehicles, including 189 455 minibuses, 25 725 buses, 294 917 motor cycles and more than one million commercial vehicles. The Transvaal accounts for 52,71% of

These flyovers near Johannesburg form part of South Africa's extensive road network

all motor vehicles, the Cape Province for 24,08%, Natal for 15,81% and the Orange Free State for 7,40%.

Since 1985 the minibus has, apart from private use, become very popular as a taxi in metropolitan areas, especially on the Witwatersrand. The vast majority of taxi permits are held by black owners or operators of these taxis. The Southern Africa Black Taxi Association (Sabta) and the South African Long Distance Taxi Association (Saldta) attempt to improve and maintain the standard of taxi drivers with a view to promoting road safety in the interest of the public. Sabta has become the largest client for spares, tyres and petrol companies and vehicle manufacturers.

In major metropolitan areas road transport services for passengers are provided by local authorities and private companies who operate scheduled bus services between peripheral areas and central points. In a new transport era these operators have been obliged to respond to changing circumstances. Unremunerative, low-demand services are rationalised while high demand routes are served more intensively. In areas where bus services are discontinued, passengers are conveyed by other modes of transport, notably minibus taxis. Inter-city bus services between major cities, such as Cape Town, Johannesburg and Durban, are well patronised.

Transnet

Transnet comprises Spoornet, Portnet, Autonet, Petronet and South African Airways. Previously known as the South African Transport Services (SATS), it was privatised on 1 April 1990. The Government remains the sole shareholder. Transnet employs 161 761 (July 1991) staff members and has fixed assets exceeding R33 500 million (1991 book value).

Railways
Spoornet operates 21 303 route km of railroads (34 110 km of track). The narrow standard gauge of 1 065 mm was dictated by the mountainous terrain between the ports and the hinterland when construction started in the last two decades of the 19th century.

The road transport service, which carried 4,5 million passengers and 3,1 million tons of goods in 1990/91 over a route distance of 111,2 million km, links outlying areas with existing railheads and trunk routes.

Altogether 42,6% of the entire rail network is electrified. Electric locomotives haul most main line passenger and goods trains (86,5%). The intensive suburban passenger services on the Witwatersrand and in Pretoria, Durban and Cape Town use electric traction exclusively. Some of the electric locomotives in service are the most powerful machines ever built for a 1 065 mm gauge railway.

Traffic-control systems and rolling stock are continually improved so that the rail network can continue to meet the growing transport needs of South Africa and much of the subcontinent. The network is divided into 10 regions. Computerised traffic control has been installed on all important main lines. A modern signalling system permits trains to be routed automatically and traffic capacity to be utilised to the limit.

Sentrarand, the computer-controlled marshalling yard for the Pretoria/Witwatersrand/Vereeniging area, was opened in September 1984. The yard comprises 20 arrival tracks, 64 classification lines, 32 departure tracks and 10 sorting lines (herring-bone yards), it is the first of four modules built at a cost of R450 million. It permits the marshalling of freight trains running directly to Durban, East London, Port Elizabeth and Cape Town. When all four phases are completed, it will be one of the largest marshalling yards in the world.

Most rolling stock is manufactured locally to suit South African conditions and demands. Goods trucks are specially designed for the particular type of commodity to be transported, namely ore, perishables, timber, grain, containers and coal. Timber-bodied passenger coaches are being replaced by steel cars which combine lightness with strength. A significant innovation in recent years has been the HS bogie, which was named after the South African engineer who invented it. The bogie permits heavier loads and much higher speeds on the narrow gauge. In 1978 a world record of 355 km/h for a 1 065 mm gauge was reached with a suburban coach fitted with an HS bogie.

In 1972 SATS commissioned two entirely new Blue Trains to usher in a new era of luxury travel. The Blue Train runs between Pretoria and Cape Town — a distance of 1 600 km — and is particularly popular among tourists.

In 1989/90, 382 million passenger journeys were undertaken and South African trains hauled 174 million tons of freight.

Ports
There are six major ports along South Africa's coastline of nearly 3 000 km, namely Durban, Richards Bay, East

London, Port Elizabeth, Cape Town and Saldanha. Less significant are Mossel Bay, Port Nolloth and Walvis Bay (a South African enclave in Namibia).

Portnet manages most of the port facilities such as handling equipment (fork-lift trucks, wharf cranes, mobile cranes and straddle carriers), cargo wharves, container terminals and sheds at these ports. It also controls the cargo-handling activities and facilities of private concerns within harbour perimeters. With the exception of private installations and stevedoring, Portnet provides all other port services (pilotage, tugs, berthing, shore labour and cargo handling). This ensures uniform tariffs and regulations, efficient services and high standards of operation, and rapid transit between the harbours and their hinterlands.

In terms of shipping and freight activity, **Durban** is South Africa's busiest port and is believed to be the third largest port in Africa. At low tide the working depth at the entrance to the 893 hectare bay is 12,7 m. The total length of commercial quayage is 15 195 m and the sheds have a floor space of approximately 92 000 square metres with a capacity of 317 000 m^3. Deep-sea and coastal ro-ro vessels can also be accommodated and there are several deep-sea and coastal container berths. Handling and transfer facilities are among the most modern. Repair facilities include the Prince Edward graving dock (352 m) and a floating dry dock (106 m).

Richards Bay was primarily built for exporting coal from the Eastern Transvaal coalfields. It is situated 190 km northeast of Durban and was commissioned in 1976. Measured in terms of freight volume, it is South Africa's biggest port. In 1987 it handled approximately 50% of all imports and exports. It can accommodate bulk carriers of up to 350 000 tons. Except for the coal berth, there are five berths for general and bulk cargo. Handling facilities include an elaborate conveyor belt system, a multipurpose, bulk-handling installation, ship loaders and unloaders, and a stacker.

The port of **Cape Town**, the oldest harbour in South

Africa, has berths for container vessels, general cargo carriers and a pier for ro-ro traffic. The precooling store, where the bulk of fruit exports is handled, has a capacity of 12 000 m^3 and is privately operated. A large percentage of the country's deciduous fruit is handled through this port. The Sturrock graving dock (360 m) is the largest in the southern hemisphere.

Main features of **Port Elizabeth** harbour are its mechanical ore-handling plant (up to 1 500 tons hourly) and the precooling store which has a capacity of 7 500 m^3. It has more than 3 400 m of quayage and a container terminal that has two berths. Vessels with a draught of up to 12 m can use the harbour.

Saldanha, about 110 km northwest of Cape Town, is the largest harbour surface area (7 434 ha) on the West Coast of Africa. Its port area is larger than that of Durban, Cape Town, Port Elizabeth and East London combined. Originally developed for exporting more than 30 million tons of iron ore annually, the ore-loading jetty can handle carriers of 350 000 tons. Handling facilities include an ore tipper, a conveyor belt system and two ship loaders (with an hourly capacity of 8 000 tons).

East London, South Africa's only river port, has traditionally handled much of the import and export traffic of countries to the north of South Africa. The main feature of this harbour on the Buffalo River is a modern grain elevator with a storage capacity of 75 300 m^3. The port also has a graving dock (198,5 m).

Transnet has built large container terminals at City Deep (Johannesburg), Bellville (Cape Town), Bayhead (Durban) and a container depot at Capital Park (Pretoria). Special container trains connect these terminals to the ports of Durban, Cape Town and Port Elizabeth.

Airways
South African Airways (SAA), the country's national carrier, is a member of the International Air Transport Association (IATA) and operates a comprehensive net-

work of services. Domestically, SAA provides more than 600 flights a week that link all major centres.

International scheduled air services are provided between the RSA and at least 32 other countries. Twenty eight foreign airlines provide scheduled air services to South Africa, providing air links between some 46 foreign points and the RSA.

During 1990/91 SAA extended its service to Nairobi, Abidjan and Kinshasa bringing the total number of destinations in Africa to 14 (12 countries) with a frequency of 41 flights a week.

SAA operates services to 10 European cities, daily services to London, a weekly flight to Manchester, and regular services to Taipei, Hong Kong and Rio de Janeiro. The strategic timetable provides for non-stop flights to three European gateways, namely Lisbon, Zurich and Frankfurt, with onward connections to Paris, Rome, Vienna, Tel Aviv, Brussels and Amsterdam. Scheduled air services between the RSA and foreign countries are arranged by formal bilateral air agreements where the respective governments nominate a carrier on the route or by informal commercial agreements. Eighteen bilateral agreements and 14 commercial agreements exist between the RSA and foreign countries. Due to the recent lifting of US sanctions, SAA reintroduced two flights a week between Johannesburg and New York on 4 November 1991. From 3 December 1991 an additional weekly flight was introduced with extra flights during the Christmas holidays.

Foreign airlines which have started new scheduled services to the RSA are: Air Zaire, Air Seychelles, Austrian Airlines, Cathay Pacific, China Airlines, Air Madagascar and Kenya Airways.

There are SAA offices in more than 50 cities in approximately 30 countries. In addition to their primary function as airline offices they also serve as information centres on tourism and business opportunities in South Africa.

In the financial year ended March 1991, SAA carried a grand total of 5 258 431 passengers compared to

5 374 337 the previous year, while 56 080 439 kg of cargo was conveyed compared with 62 645 222 kg the previous year.

There are 224 licensed aerodromes and heliports in South Africa. The main international airport is Jan Smuts, near Johannesburg. Others are Louis Botha (Durban) and D F Malan (Cape Town).

Civil aviation

The Department of Transport administers the following state airports: Jan Smuts Airport (Johannesburg), D F Malan Airport (Cape Town), Louis Botha Airport (Durban), H F Verwoerd Airport (Port Elizabeth), J B M Hertzog Airport (Bloemfontein), Ben Schoeman Airport (East London), P W Botha Airport (George), B J Vorster Airport (Kimberley) and Pierre van Ryneveld Airport (Upington). These airports handled a total of more than 12 million passengers in 1990.

Aviation in South Africa is governed in terms of various Acts administered by the Commissioner of Civil Aviation under the direction of the Director-General for Transport.

The Chief Directorate: Civil Aviation consists of four directorates, namely airport systems and development, aviation safety, aviation administration and air traffic control.

The **airport systems and development directorate** is primarily concerned with planning and developing state airports, navigation and communication aids, and security systems. A team of engineers and technicians keeps abreast of the latest developments and regularly undertakes training tours abroad. Besides planning and development, this directorate also supplies electrical and avionic maintenance services at all state airports.

The **aviation safety directorate** consists of three divisions, namely airworthiness, flight services and accident investigation.

In the airworthiness division trained engineers and technicians strictly enforce International Civil Aviation

Organisation (ICAO) stipulations. South Africa is a member of ICAO.

The flight services division ensures that pilot training and operations conform to ICAO standards. The accident investigation division records and investigates accidents and incidents in the interests of aviation safety.

The **aviation administration directorate** covers a very wide field. It is responsible for, among other things, procuring and administering staff, economic activities, fiscal planning, cleaning services, fire-fighting services, control measures, security services, passenger services and information.

A subdivision deals with specialised administration such as applications from local and foreign airlines to operate in South Africa (National Transport Commission), licensing of airlines and training institutions, amendments to regulations and Acts, subsidies to local authorities for developing airfields and financial assistance with flight training, search and rescue services and aid to the National Sea Rescue Institute, special flights and authorisation for such flights, and pilot licensing and examination.

The **air traffic control directorate** deals with the control and supply of advice and information in respect of all airspace. The head office component is geared to research and development of air traffic and control measures, and must ensure that it keeps abreast of the latest developments regarding communication. The ICAO also prescribes requirements in this respect.

The rapid development in civil aviation is reflected in the following table:

	1989	1990
Private pilots	4 187	4 760
Commercial pilots	894	1 001
Senior commercial pilots	43	55
Airline transport pilots	735	937
Registered aircraft	4 341	5 399
Freight cargo (kilograms)	208 749 000	218 674 000
Passenger transport (state airports)	11 288 800	12 217 300
Aircraft movements (state airports)	283 148	316 588

There are 19 private airlines who employ a variety of aircraft to operate scheduled air services to link South Africa's smaller towns with its cities. Other non-scheduled flights are offered countrywide by about 123 operators.

In terms of the deregulated Domestic Air Services Act the National Transport Commission granted a licence to Trek Airways (Flitestar) on 14 December 1990 to operate on the main trunk routes within the RSA. As with any airline operator Flitestar was required to obtain an operating certificate from the Department of Transport. The operating certificate is issued once the Department is satisfied that an applicant's intended operation is safe. Steps have been taken to accommodate Flitestar at the following state airports: Jan Smuts, D F Malan, Louis Botha and H F Verwoerd. The first flight was between Johannesburg and Cape Town on 16 October 1991.

COMMUNICATION

Radio and television

The South African Broadcasting Corporation (SABC) is a utility corporation which was established in 1936. Its radio services include:

— *Radio Suid-Afrika*, a full-spectrum radio service in Afrikaans — 140 broadcasting hours weekly
— Radio South Africa, a full-spectrum service in English — 140 broadcasting hours weekly
— six regional Afrikaans/English commercial services — Radio Highveld Stereo, Good Hope Stereo, Port Natal Stereo, Jacaranda, Oranje and Algoa — 133 broadcasting hours weekly
— Radio Lotus, an Indian cultural service broadcasts in English, 133 hours weekly
— Radio 5, a youth-orientated commercial service — broadcasts in English and Afrikaans, 133 hours weekly in stereo
— Radio RSA: The Voice of South Africa — 177 broadcasting hours a week; to Africa on short wave in English, Portuguese, French, Tsonga, Lozi, Swahili and Chichewa
— nine public services (Radio Sesotho, Lebowa, Zulu, Xhosa, Setswana, Tsonga, Venda, Ndebele and Swazi)
— Radio Metro, a 24-hour a day programme in English for urban black listeners
— Radio Orion, an all-night FM music station — 42 broadcasting hours weekly
— Radio 2000, a countrywide facility service, mainly for religious, educational and sports programmes, soothing music and TV simulcasts — 139 broadcasting hours weekly.

The SABC offers television viewers four services in seven languages: TV1 in English and Afrikaans for about 120 hours weekly; TV2 in Zulu and Xhosa for 59 hours weekly; TV3 in South Sotho, North Sotho and

Tswana for 59 hours weekly, and TV4 in English and Afrikaans for 27 hours weekly.

Up to 8% of air time on all channels is devoted to advertising. The annual (1991) television licence fee per household is R 150, regardless of the number of receivers owned. Radio licence fees were abolished in 1982.

According to Amps '91, TV1 attracts about 5,23 million viewers, TV2 and TV3 about 4,09 million, and TV4 about 3,5 million, during the available broadcasting time.

M-Net is a subscription television service run by a consortium of newspaper publishing houses. It broadcasts both in encoded form via decoders to monthly subscribers and unencoded form to the general public during an 'open time' window. It was started in October 1986 and currently has more than 600 000 subscribers. It has launched two new services, East-Net for Indian viewers and Canal Português for Portuguese subscribers, as well as a special channel for children, K-TV. The M-Net signal covers all the major metropolitan areas and, with the recent introduction of its satellite service, also several smaller rural areas.

Christian Television (CTV), which was founded in 1990 started broadcasting on TV1 and TV4 in June 1991.

Telephones
There are more than three million main telephone services in South Africa, of which 96,44% are connected to 1 072 automatic exchanges. A network of more than 6 306 connections comprising overland lines, submarine cables and satellite rings enables South African subscribers to dial directly to 205 of the 207 international destinations where services exist. An extensive domestic trunk network of open-wire carriers, microwave, coaxial cable and other systems provides over 50,7 million km of high-quality speech channels to link cities, towns and villages throughout the country.

The Hartebeesthoek satellite station near Pretoria

The existing electro-mechanical switching system is increasingly being replaced by a fully electronic system.

South Africa's international telephone service developed from a single-circuit radio-telephone link to Britain in the mid-1930s. The South Atlantic Telecommunications (SAT-1) cable was laid in the 1960s over a distance of 10 000 km between South Africa and Portugal and subsequently linked to other submarine cables. Three satellite earth stations at Hartebeesthoek in the Transvaal link South Africa with the Intelsat Atlantic and Indian Ocean communication satellite systems and also provide back-up facilities in case the SAT-1 cable breaks down. Overseas calls dialled directly via the cable or the satellite systems are routed through the automatic international exchange in Johannesburg. Manually operated international calls are routed through Cape Town.

Telex and fax services

Because of a substantial increase in the use of telefax services the utilisation of the telex and teletex services has declined.

The inland telex service in South Africa is fully automatic. At the end of March 1991 there were 13 914 telex subscribers who had direct access to subscribers in 198 destinations via the automatic international exchange. A further four destinations can be reached through the manual exchange in Johannesburg.

A teletex service capable of transmitting 40 times faster than telex, was introduced in 1983. By March 1991 there were 1 988 teletex subscribers. A teletex subscriber can communicate with other teletex subscribers locally and abroad as well as with any telex subscriber anywhere in the world.

Data transmission was introduced in 1965 and is now carried by leased line (at standard speeds of up to 9 600 bits a second), the public telephone network (up to 9 600 bits a second in all centres), the switched data network of the Post Office's Saponet system (up to 48 000 bits a second) or through high-quality communication point-to-point links (up to 64 000 bits a second) provided on a new public digital data network (Diginet) commissioned in March 1986. Diginet-Plus now offers data transmission at speeds of up to and including 1,92 Mbps. International data transmission is provided through the packet switching service which operates via Saponet (up to 64 000 bits a second): leased lines (up to 56 000 bits a second), or on a dial-up basis (up to 2 400 bits a second). The private sector is permitted to supply approved data modems under licence to Post Office clients. By 31 March 1991, 48 681 data modems supplied by the Post Office, were in use.

Telegraph services

Altogether 888 post offices in South Africa have access to a computerised telegram retransmission system which operates on the store-and-forward principle. The system stores the telegrams and automatically re-transmits them in order of priority to destinations in South Africa and neighbouring countries, as well as to the overseas countries to which South Africa has direct telegraph services.

Postal services

The Post Office handles about 7,8 million articles of mail every working day. It uses all forms of transport — national and commercial airlines, the rail and road motor services of Transnet, motor vehicles of the Post Office or private contractors, even bicycles — to convey mail to even the most distant parts of the country. Standardised mail articles are automatically carried by air for at least a part of the journey. Letter-sorting machines in Cape Town, Durban, Johannesburg and Pretoria can encode and sort letters addressed by typewriters and computers at an hourly rate of 30 000. These machines sort mail by means of a four-digit postal code.

Direct surface mail is dispatched to 74 countries and received from 64 others while direct air mail is dispatched to 50 countries and received from 63 others. Mail for other destinations is forwarded through one or more of these countries. Ocean mail is carried to all parts of the globe by the first available ship.

Overseas air mail is conveyed chiefly by South African Airways, but also by 21 international airlines operating regularly to and from Jan Smuts Airport, Johannesburg.

The press

More than 5 000 newspapers, periodicals and journals are published regularly. The technology employed by the local press is completely modern, largely because it has to maintain international standards to compete with overseas publications imported freely into the country. A total of 63 new publications were registered in 1990.

There are four major press groups. The Argus Printing and Publishing Company (six dailies, two Sundays,

Main newspapers (mid-1991)

Name	City of publication	Frequency	Language	Audited circulation
Beeld	Johannesburg	M	A	99 909
Business Day	Johannesburg	M	E	33 582
City Press	Johannesburg	Sun	E	134 732
Daily Dispatch	East London	M	E	35 050
Diamond Fields Advertiser	Kimberley	M	E	8 207
Die Burger	Cape Town	M	A	86 515
Die Transvaler	Johannesburg	M	A	49 121
Die Volksblad	Bloemfontein	A	A	24 780
EP Herald	Port Elizabeth	M	E	29 900
Evening Post	Port Elizabeth	A	E	23 166
Ilanga	Durban	Bi-W	Z & E	124 552
Imvo Zabantsundu	King William's Town	Sat	X & E	37 302
Oosterlig	Port Elizabeth	M	A	9 280
New Nation	Johannesburg	W/E	E	70 223

Post (Natal)	Durban	Sun	E	48 906
Pretoria News	Pretoria	A	E	25 751
Rapport	Johannesburg	Sun	A	362 272
Sowetan	Johannesburg	M	E	184 401
Sunday Star	Johannesburg	Sun	E	100 143
Sunday Times	Johannesburg	Sun	E	520 844
Sunday Tribune	Durban	Sun	E	126 565
The Argus	Cape Town	A	E	103 368
The Cape Times	Cape Town	M	E	55 894
The Citizen	Johannesburg	M	E	140 435
The Daily News	Durban	A	E	98 467
The Natal Mercury	Durban	M	E	63 109
The Natal Witness	Pietermaritzburg	M	E	28 610
The Star	Johannesburg	24h	E	235 128
Weekly Mail	Excom	W/E	E	27 157

M (morning daily), A (afternoon daily), Sun (Sunday), Sat (Saturday), W/E (week-end edition), Bi-W (bi-weekly), 24h (24 hours), Z (Zulu), X (Xhosa), E (English), A (Afrikaans) one bi-weekly and one weekly paper); Times Media Limited (four dailies and two Sundays); Nasionale Media (four dailies, one Sunday, several country papers and a family of consumer magazines), and Perskor (two dailies, several country papers and consumer magazines).

Foreign news agencies represented in South Africa are Agence-France Presse, Associated Press, United Press International, Deutsche Presse-Agentur and Reuters Economic Services. Several large foreign newspapers, and radio and television stations also have local representatives. The South African Press Association (Sapa) is South Africa's own national news agency. It transmits approximately 100 000 words of foreign and domestic news each day to its member publications, which include virtually all daily and Sunday papers.

Despite limited statutory restrictions on the press and additional temporary curbs in times of national emergency, the South African press enjoys a great measure of freedom. Restraints on the press include those relating to certain aspects of defence, prisons, police matters and divorce proceedings in court.

All member publications of the Newspaper Press Union (NPU) voluntarily comply with the code of conduct laid down by the Media Council. The Council consists of a retired judge and representatives of the press and public, and hears complaints against the press. NPU members are specifically excluded from the provisions of the Publications Act of 1974.

Censorship

All publications, except newspapers registered with the NPU (see above), films and other forms of public entertainment are subject to control in terms of the Publications Act of 1974, which seeks to prevent the display or publication of material that is obscene, blasphemous, harmful to public morals or the safety and good order of the State, or contemptuous of any one section of the population. The Act provides for Publications Committees consisting of knowledgeable members of the public to judge publications and entertainments submitted to them, and a special Appeal Board to hear appeals against the decisions of these committees. Since publications and media control reflect the wishes of the communities they serve, a greater openness is now prevalent.

EDUCATION

Over the years the cultural diversity of South Africans has imposed strong demands on the educational system in the country. Officially, mother tongue education is still regarded as a priority, but its implementation is exacting in a country where at least 24 different languages are spoken. The whole education system is constantly under review and the authorities are open to suggestions for the broader, ongoing restructuring of education.

In 1984, a new educational system was established which was partially based on an in-depth investigation conducted by the Human Sciences Research Council (HSRC) in 1981; a White Paper by the Government, released in November 1983, and the South African Constitution of 1983. The National Policy for General Education Affairs Act of 1984 provided for the creation of a new Department of National Education which would determine and monitor national educational policy for all departments of education in the following areas:

— norms and standards for the financing of running and capital costs of education for all
— salaries and conditions of employment of staff
— the professional registration of teachers
— norms and standards for syllabuses and examinations, and for certification of qualifications.

In terms of the Constitution, education is an own affair — each population group has its own education department. Provision is, however, made for the rendering of services by one group to another.

The majority of South African pupils attend government schools, which are administered by the national departments of education. However, private schools run by church denominations or private enterprise are an increasingly important feature of the education system. Pupils in private schools follow the same syllabuses as pupils in government schools. Education standards, especially regarding syllabuses and examinations, are the same for all departmental schools. Furthermore, the same nationally recognised certificates are issued for trade training and advanced technical education.

At school level, education is compulsory for Indians, coloureds and whites, and the State assumes full financial responsibility for their schooling. About 80% of all black children of school-going age are at school.

Library, guidance, medical, psychological, sports, audio-visual and testing services are provided. Specialised education is also provided for disabled children and for those with learning disabilities.

Pre-tertiary training

The present system of differentiated education offers a 12-year school programme grouped into phases. The first nine years of schooling, that is, the junior primary, senior primary and junior secondary phases are devoted mainly to developing basic skills and the knowledge required for the successful continuation of education in the next phase. During the senior secondary phase, differentiation continues vertically with subjects offered at higher, lower and standard grade. A wide range of subjects allows pupils to select subjects in accordance with their interests and abilities. Pre-primary education is offered mainly in privately owned nursery schools subsidised by the State, although some pre-primary schools are run by education departments.

Courses for post-school, but pre-tertiary, training are conducted by technical colleges and various other establishments, including a number of correspondence colleges. Candidates who successfully complete these courses obtain National Certificates.

Tertiary education

Tertiary and vocational education is offered at universities, technikons, colleges of education and a number of other institutions. At present there are 11 residential technikons. In addition, Technikon RSA offers voca-

The provision of sufficient educational facilities is a top priority

tional tuition by correspondence. A large variety of technical, commercial and other types of courses, which lead to National and Higher National Diplomas, are offered by the technikons on a full-time or part-time basis.

Each education department administers its own external or internal examinations, but university admission is controlled by the Joint Matriculation Board. All universities are autonomous institutions subsidised by the State. At present there are 17 residential universities. The University of South Africa (Unisa) teaches through correspondence. Vista University, which was established in 1981, is the most recently established university. This multicampus institution offers courses on a decentralised basis in the metropolitan areas. It became operational in 1983 with four local campuses and an additional campus for the further training of teachers.

Teacher training is provided by the universities as well as by the colleges of education of the various education departments. Universities, however, mainly produce teachers qualified to teach at secondary schools.

Changing the system

In the spirit of the Government's reform initiatives, the various education departments have already instituted several changes. During 1990 the Department of Education and Culture: House of Assembly, which is mainly responsible for providing education to the white population group, announced its additional models for the provision of education. These additional models were established as a mechanism whereby school communities could, if they so desired, exercise a greater degree of responsibility for the management of their own schools, which includes the determination of their own admissions policy. In terms of this, pupils of other population groups may be admitted to schools which previously only admitted white children. The three additional models for the provision of education are:

— Model A: A private school established in the existing building after the closure of an ordinary government school.
— Model B: An ordinary government school which determines its own admissions policy within the provisions of the Constitution.
— Model C: An ordinary government school which has been declared a state-aided school.

By choosing one of the additional models, about 30% of the schools under the jurisdiction of the Department of Education and Culture: House of Assembly have accepted the devolved authority to determine, among other matters, their own admissions policies.

The single largest problem encountered in education at present is the financing of a system which is growing annually at a rate of about 4,4% while the economic growth of the country is less than 1% per annum. It is therefore not surprising that on average the real per capita expenditure on education is decreasing. In the long run this can only result in the lowering of standards. Substantial backlogs, especially as far as school buildings are concerned, exist within black education. The elimination, or even a significant reduction of these backlogs will take thousands of millions of rands. Over the last two years about R1 000 million was allocated and spent for the specific purpose of tackling this task.

When it became evident that a completely new strategy was necessary to provide affordable education without lowering the standard of education, the Minister of National Education announced on 18 May 1990 that the Committee of Heads of Education Departments was engaged in an investigation into a comprehensive education renewal strategy. The aim of the investigation was to address some of the most crucial problems in education. For this purpose working groups, consisting of senior specialists from education departments, the organised teaching profession, and universities and technikons were established.

In the course of their investigations the working groups had access to more than 200 submissions. These recommendations were made to the Committee of Heads of Education Departments by individuals and institutions from within and outside the education system and who were invited to do so. A discussion document containing about 70 proposals was published in June 1991 and a draft model for South African education into the future was published on 21 November 1991. Marked changes in the education system; greater involvement by the private sector especially in non-formal education, and the establishment of an alternative type of institution on the post-secondary level to accommodate the thousands of students emerging from secondary education who cannot be admitted directly to universities and technikons, are envisaged.

A comparison of the number of pupils and students educated in general and technical courses at the different educational institutions during 1989 and 1990

	Schools		Technical colleges		Colleges of Education		Technikons		Universities	
	1989	1990	1989	1990	1989	1990	1989	1990	1989	1990
Whites	977 411	971 587	45 694	48 852	10 714	9 467	47 662	53 795	156 737	153 807
Indians	241 749	242 323	5 882	5 976	1 235	734	5 558	5 864	19 179	18 854
Coloureds	852 235	847 647	4 160	4 625	8 331	7 636	5 444	6 942	18 968	18 112
Blacks	5 136 435	5 484 998	9 638	12 721	32 322	32 247	9 654	16 823	91 462	96 137
TOTAL	7 207 830	7 546 555	65 374	72 174	52 602	50 084	68 318	83 424	286 346	286 910

Note: These figures exclude Transkei, Bophuthatswana, Venda and Ciskei
Source: Department of National Education

CULTURE

South Africa offers vital and diverse cultural fare. The country's artists are active both locally and abroad in the fields of theatre, classical and modern music, opera, ballet, the visual arts and literature (drama, poetry and prose). Many South African productions are showcased on stage and at exhibitions abroad.

One of the many highlights on the South African arts calendar is an annual national festival of the arts in Grahamstown. Participants are more often than not subsequently invited to take their shows from Grahamstown to well-known festivals abroad. The Standard Bank Young Artists Award for Fine Art is also presented at the festival.

The Roodepoort International Eisteddfod, held during the first week in October every second year since 1981, attracts individual performers and troupes from all over the world to its festival of song and dance on the shores of the Roodepoort Lake near Johannesburg.

Performing arts

A state-subsidised performing arts council in each of the four provinces professionally promotes theatre, opera, ballet and music. The South African Coordinating Performing Arts Council (Sacpac) is the umbrella organisation established to promote the interests of these four councils. The Performing Arts Council of the Transvaal (Pact), the Cape Performing Arts Board (Capab), the Performing Arts Council of the Orange Free State (Pacofs) and the Natal Performing Arts Council (Napac), employ more than 2 000 artists and theatre technicians and annually stage about 5 000 performances in urban and country areas. Annual box-office turnover is approximately R 58 million. Much valuable work is done to promote culture in a community context.

Prestigious theatre complexes, comparable to any modern theatre in the world, are the Nico Malan

Theatre in Cape Town, the State Theatre in Pretoria, the Civic Theatre in Johannesburg, the Sand du Plessis Theatre in Bloemfontein, and the Natal Playhouse in Durban. Adequate multipurpose theatres are available in other major cities and larger towns.

Commercial theatre is also well established, particularly in cities such as Johannesburg, Durban, Port Elizabeth and Cape Town.

South Africa has produced a remarkable number of ballet dancers and choreographers of world standing. Some of them turn to the stages and concert halls of America and Europe to further their careers and to make a name for themselves. Among the best-known ballet dancers who have worked both locally and abroad are John Cranko, Nadia Nerina, David Poole, Dulcie Howes, Deanne Bergsma, Johaar Mosaval, Monica Mason and Vivian Lorrayne. The ballet schools of the performing arts councils do sterling work in promoting the art of ballet.

South African opera singers such as Marieta Napier, Emma Renzi, Mimi Coertse, Nellie du Toit and Elisabeth Connel have a worldwide reputation, and have at various times graced the opera stages of New York, Bayreuth, Milan, Vienna, London, Sydney and elsewhere. All the best-known operas have been staged to great acclaim in South Africa. International stars are imported from time to time, but most roles are filled with distinction by local artists.

There are six main orchestras, namely the South African Broadcasting Corporation (SABC) Orchestra, Pact's Transvaal Philharmonic Orchestra, the Cape Town Symphony Orchestra, the Capab Orchestra, the Natal Philharmonic Orchestra and the OFS Symphony Orchestra. A number of city and outstanding youth orchestras, independent of the arts councils, and many amateur and semi-professional orchestras regularly give performances in the major centres. Folk-dancing and music are performed by special interest groups. Several local choirs, including school and children's choirs, have won international competitions.

Jazz and pop music have a large local following. Well-known popular music artists such as Brenda Fassie, Lucky Dube, Sello 'Chicco' Twala, Yvonne Chaka-Chaka, Steve Kekana and Sipho 'Hotstix' Mabuse have made a name for themselves locally and are well-received overseas and in the rest of Africa. There is a lively audience for popular Afrikaans and English entertainers.

In the current relaxed cultural climate, a new kind of music has emerged in the country — a synthesis of black and white sounds. This vibrant new music is finding extensive international favour and more and more groups — for example Ladysmith Black Mambaso, Johnny Clegg and Savuka, and Mango Groove — whose musical expression reflects both African and European elements, are touring through Europe, the United States, the Soviet Union and the Far East.

Literature

South African authors writing in English (drama, poetry and prose) have won international recognition. Afrikaans literature, especially poetry is prolific and is often translated. South African English authors of note include Sarah Gertrude Millin, Laurens van der Post, Stuart Cloete, Alan Paton, Olive Schreiner, Doris Lessing, Alex la Guma, Jack Cope, Dan Jacobson, J M Coetzee, Nadine Gordimer (1991 Nobel Prize for Literature), B M Malefo, Gibson Kente, Maishe Maponya, Matsemala Manaka, Mbongeni Ngema, Zakes Mda, Athol Fugard (playwright), Roy Campbell and Oswald Mtshali (poets).

Poets whose work represents milestones in the development of Afrikaans literature include Eugéne Marais, C Louis Leipoldt, the brothers W E G and N P van Wyk Louw, Uys Krige, Elisabeth Eybers, Sheila Cussons, D J Opperman and Breyten Breytenbach. A new generation of authors is attracting wide attention. Well-known novelists include D F Malherbe, J van Melle, Etienne Leroux, André P Brink, Elsa Joubert,

Breyten Breytenbach, Chris Barnard, Dalene Matthee and Hennie Aucamp. Playwrights of note include Adam Small, P G du Plessis, André P Brink, Chris Barnard, N P van Wyk Louw and Uys Krige.

Various prestigious literary prizes such as the Hertzog Prize, the CNA Award, the Thomas Pringle Award and the Olive Schreiner Prize are awarded each year.

Visual arts
Among South Africa's greatest art treasures are the approximately 3 000 rock art sites where Stone Age Bushmen recorded scenes from their daily lives. Most of these are protected by the National Monuments Act of 1969.

The sculptor, Samson Makwala, with one of his works of art

A list of South Africa's better-known modern painters, sculptors and ceramic artists would include about 200 names, many of whom studied abroad. Collections of South African art, including child art, are regularly exhibited overseas.

There are art galleries and museums of various types in all major centres. Important collections of Africana include the Strange Collection in Johannesburg and the William Fehr Collection in Cape Town, as well as collections in the Africana Museum in Johannesburg, the Koopmans de Wet House in Cape Town and the National Cultural History and Open-Air Museum in Pretoria.

Important art awards are the annual Volkskas Atelier Competition, the AA Life Vita Award and the Cape Town Triennial.

Cultural organisations

Numerous cultural organisations are active in various fields. Two of the best known are the *Suid-Afrikaanse Akademie vir Wetenskap en Kuns* (Academy for Science and Art) which promotes Afrikaans language, literature, art and science, and the English Academy of Southern Africa which promotes English and English-based culture on the subcontinent.

Cinema

Because the South African market is too small for the production of feature films to be economical, the Government introduced a subsidy system for the local industry in 1956, the output of which is modest by world standards. There are about 500 cinemas and 40 drive-in theatres countrywide. Foreign film companies make feature films in South Africa from time to time — either independently or as co-productions with local producers.

A new emphasis is being placed on the so-called art films and various film festivals regularly show selected foreign and local productions.

Architecture

The oldest traces of man-made environments, dating from the Iron Age, are found in the low areas of the Transvaal and Natal. These traces consist of stone walls and traditional hut patterns.

The Cape-Dutch style of architecture which evolved from European roots and was adapted to the local climate and building materials, is uniquely South African. Its characteristics are thick whitewashed walls, gables, a large rectangular front room leading directly from a raised verandah running the length of the house and flanked at each end by a low brick seat. Thatch was originally used as roofing material.

Towards the end of the 18th century, lasting contributions were made in the Cape by Anton Anreith, a German sculptor, and Louis Thibault, a French architect.

Towards the end of the 19th century the developments resulting from the discovery of diamonds and gold attracted many architects from overseas. In Natal several fine buildings were designed by Philip Dudgeon and in the Transvaal a Dutch architect, Sytze Wierda, was active.

Sir Herbert Baker dominated the first decade of the 20th century. Among his designs are the impressive Union Buildings overlooking Pretoria and South Africa House in London.

The influence of Louis Kahn and the American school tend currently to dominate, and most new commercial and other buildings are in a contemporary style.

RELIGION

Almost 80% of South Africans profess Christianity, while about five million still adhere to traditional African or tribal religions. Other major religious groups are the Hindus, Muslims and Jews, in that order. A sizeable minority have no religious affiliations. There is complete freedom of worship. Official policy is one of non-interference in religious practices.

Christian churches

The largest single religious grouping is the Black Independent Church movement, which includes nearly one in three of all black believers. This means that the 4 000 independent churches have more than seven million members. The movement covers the whole spectrum of orthodoxy and heterodoxy. In Northern Natal/KwaZulu and the Southeastern Transvaal they outnumber all other religious groups combined.

The Dutch Reformed (*Nederduitse Gereformeerde*) family of churches is the largest of the established churches. It has about four million adherents within the borders of South Africa. Extensive missionary work is done in various African countries and overseas.

The Catholic Church, with almost three million followers, is the third largest Christian group and the largest established church among blacks, who constitute 75% of its total membership.

The Methodist Church of Southern Africa, which grew from British Methodism, recently installed its first ever bishop. Methodism, as is the case with most other denominations, grew as a result of the establishment of missions throughout Southern Africa.

The largest Anglican Church in South Africa is the Church of the Province of Southern Africa. It is the fourth largest of the established church families and has almost two million members.

The first Lutheran congregation was established in

The religious affiliation of the SA population

Religious group	Number in thousands	Percentage
African indigenous churches	7 006	22,75
Nederduitse Gereformeerde Church (NGK)	4 299	13,96
Roman Catholic Church	2 963	9,62
Methodist Church	2 747	8,92
Anglican Church (Church of the Province)	2 026	6,58
Lutheran Church	1 093	3,55
Presbyterian Church	758	2,46
Congregational churches	607	1,97
Nederduitse Hervormde Church (NHK)	357	1,16
Apostolic Faith Mission	351	1,14
Baptist Church	317	1,03
Gereformeerde Church (GK)	243	0,79
Full Gospel Church	228	0,74
Assemblies of God	179	0,58
Seventh Day Adventists	102	0,33
Other Christian churches	773	2,51
TOTAL: CHRISTIAN CHURCHES	24 052	78,09
Hindus	650	2,11
Muslims	434	1,41
Judaists	148	0,48
Other non-Christians	5 513	17,90
TOTAL: NON-CHRISTIANS	6 748	21,91
TOTAL POPULATION	30 797	100,00

Source: The religious percentage for the population groups were taken from the latest religious census of 1980 (Report no. 02-08-06) and are assumed not to have changed significantly
The total populations for the different groups are the mid-year estimates of the Central Statistical Services for 1990

A baptismal ceremony at the seaside

Cape Town in 1780. Numerous congregations have been founded among Asian, black and coloured communities.

Some other Christian denominations include the Anglican Church of England in South Africa, Presbyterian Church, United Congregational Church of Southern Africa, Gereformeerde Kerk, Nederduitsch Hervormde Kerk, Apostolic Faith Mission, Full Gospel Church, Baptist Union of Southern Africa, Afrikaans Baptist Church, Assemblies of God, Salvation Army, New Apostolic Church, Greek Orthodox Church, Pentecostal Protestant Church, Seventh Day Adventist Church, Church of Christ Scientist, the Afrikaanse Protestantse Kerk and several charismatic churches. The charismatic and Pentecostal churches show a steady increase and form part of umbrella bodies, such as the International Fellowship of Christian Churches (IFCC) and the Church Alliance of Southern Africa.

HEALTH, SOCIAL WELFARE AND POPULATION DEVELOPMENT

Health

South Africa spends approximately 6,4% of its gross national product on health care. The comparative figure for developing countries is between 2% and 3%, and for developed countries between 5% and 10%. The objective of South Africa's health authorities is to provide a balanced and comprehensive service within reach of the entire population by optimal use of available resources.

In 1990/91 the total national budget for health services amounted to R 7 040 million.

Public health care funding, which comprises approximately 55% of health care and 80% of hospital beds, caters mainly for the lower income groups.

Public health care is financed by the Government from general taxes. Indigent people receive free treatment while non-indigent people are charged a tariff calculated on a sliding scale according to their taxable income. On the lowest paying scale patients pay R 21 (about US $7.30) upon admission. This fee covers all treatment and medication, irrespective of the cost or length of stay. The lowest tariff for outpatients is R 10 (about US $3.50).

The first point of contact with the public health care system is normally a primary health care clinic, from where the patient may be referred for sophisticated medical care to a community, regional or academic hospital. The health services in the rural areas are generally more basic than those found in the urban areas. Rural dwellers have access to higher levels of care via the referral system.

Private health funding constitutes approximately 45%

144

of total health expenditure. Of this amount, 60% is funded by medical schemes. In most cases the latter is subsidised by employers. The point of entry to this system is usually a private general practitioner, who refers a patient to a private medical specialist when necessary. Hospitalisation is usually in a private hospital.

Of the total population, 23% is covered by medical schemes.

Emergency treatment is provided at all public hospitals and at some private hospitals. In many countries the need for general hospital beds is decreasing. Factors that influence this tendency are improved primary health care, a reduction in the average length of hospital stay per patient, and increased outpatient and home care. In keeping with this general trend, the South African health authorities have set a norm of two to four acute general hospital beds per 1 000 of the population. In addition, long-stay and psychiatric beds are also required. There were altogether 145 778 hospital beds available in South Africa in 1990, giving a rate of 4,7 per 1 000 of the population.

The South African health care system comprises various health departments at local, provincial and central level.

Local health departments provide promotive, preventive and community health services, water, sanitary and refuse services. The implementation of general environmental and local health regulations, for example the hygienic preparation and handling of foodstuffs, also falls under their jurisdiction.

The hospital services division of the four provincial administrations provide and manage curative hospital and allied services, and to a lesser extent also primary and preventive care on a non-racial basis. The larger hospitals have facilities for all medical procedures. Most provincial hospitals also conduct outpatient clinics.

The main function of the Department of National Health and Population Development is coordination, policy-formulation, planning and the monitoring of the general health situation. Health matters of national concern such as the control of environmental hazards, implementation of a genetic service and communicable diseases such as Aids are also the responsibility of this Department.

South Africa is relatively free from the tropical diseases usually associated with Africa.

In order to facilitate co-operation and coordination between the various health service authorities, a Council for Health Policy was formed with the aim of determining national health objectives and priorities.

In 1990, 1 252 medical interns, 23 139 medical practitioners, 3 775 dentists, 6 337 medical specialists, 297 dental specialists, 26 225 qualified supplementary

Mobile clinics are used to reach patients in remote rural areas and also in densely populated areas where hospitals and clinics are not within easy reach

health services personnel, 6 253 medical students and 823 dental students were registered with the South African Medical and Dental Council. Boards have been established under the aegis of the Council for controlling the supplementary health professions.

The South African Nursing Council controls the nursing profession. In 1990 a total of 148 558 nurses and/or midwives, and nursing assistants and 17 855 student and pupil nurses were registered or enrolled with the South African Nursing Council.

The South African Pharmacy Board controls the pharmacy profession.

The disease patterns prevalent in South Africa mirror the local developmental stages of the various communities. So-called First World diseases such as Ischaemic Heart Disease among the Indian and white populations are similar in prevalence to Europe.

About 235 new Aids cases have been reported (November 1991) since the beginning of 1991 bringing the total of reported Aids cases in South Africa to 893. Carefully planned scientific surveys suggest that at least 100 000 persons are already infected and that an additional 300 people are becoming infected every day. On 24 October 1990 the Cabinet approved the establishment of an interdepartmental committee to combat Aids at national level. An Aids Unit was established whose function it is to draw up appropriate and relevant long-term strategies and to coordinate HIV-prevention efforts. The National Aids Strategy has been adopted as the country's official strategy, and an Aids Advisory Group has been established. The Unit will introduce Aids prevention education to all children in the country.

As the transfer of information worldwide has not lead to a long-term change in sexual practices, the Unit has also drawn up a communication strategy to be launched in three phases — short, medium and long term — aimed at the creation of appropriate sexual behaviour. Since such a change may take a long time, the long-term communication strategy will extend over 30 years.

So-called Third World disease patterns, with a high

proportion due to infectious diseases, are found in the outlying rural areas and in informal settlements in urban areas.

However, a large section of the population has already progressed to an intermediate stage of disease pattern, moving from mainly infectious diseases to the degenerate diseases associated with a Western lifestyle and an ageing population. Concomitant with this epidemiological trend, genetic/congenital disorders are also gaining greater relative importance. A comprehensive genetic service is provided to cope with the existing and growing need.

In 1991 a programme was developed by the Department of National Health and Population Development as part of the Government's nutritional programme to counter diseases resulting from malnutrition. For this purpose considerable resources are made available to welfare organisations, churches, provincial and local authorities.

Due to substantial improvements in the general health of South Africans, the life expectancy of the people has already (1991) passed the target of 60 years set by the World Health Organisation for the year 2000.

Research
Medical research is carried out mainly by the South African Medical Research Council (MRC), the South African Institute for Medical Research (SAIMR) and the Department of National Health and Population Development. In 1990 the MRC reorganised its research priorities into two groups. One group focuses on community health research and the other on clinical and experimental research. It also supports research at universities. The SAIMR is divided into four sections — research, diagnostic laboratory services, production (sera and vaccines) and teaching. Institutes and laboratories of the Department of National Health and Population Development carry out extensive research in the fields of occupational health, viral and tropical diseases, and the development and production of vac-

cines. They also provide a diagnostic service. The forensic and chemical laboratories play a vital role in medicolegal matters, the latter also provides a service in terms of the Foodstuffs, Cosmetics and Disinfectants Act of 1972. Human genetic disorders are closely monitored and diagnostic and counselling services provided.

The National Institute for Virology and the National Institute for Tropical Diseases carry out advanced research. The National Institute for Virology also produces vaccines, as does the State Vaccine Institute in Cape Town. Rabies and measles vaccines are imported. The State Vaccine Institute checks all imported vaccines for quality.

Social Welfare

South Africa's social welfare services have always been rendered in partnership between the private and public sectors. As far as possible, those in need are cared for by private welfare organisations with financial and other support from the State, whenever necessary.

The following are the main fields in which welfare services are being rendered: family and child care; care for the aged; care for the disabled; social security; alcohol and drug abuse, and corrective services.

The State is primarily responsible for the payment of social grants in aid, such as old-age pensions and disability grants. The National Welfare Act of 1978 called into being the South African Welfare Council, regional welfare boards and welfare committees to promote and coordinate welfare services and to involve communities in the provision of such services.

Other welfare legislation of significance is the Child Care Act of 1983 which makes provision for children in need of care, adoptions and control over child labour.

The Abuse of Dependence-producing Substances and Rehabilitation Centres Act of 1971 prohibits the dealing in and use of illegal drugs and provides for the establishment of rehabilitation centres, and the treatment of alcoholics and drug addicts. The National Advisory Board on Rehabilitation Matters functions in terms of the Act.

In 1991, 7 242 social workers and 571 student social workers in their final year were registered with the South African Council for Social Work. The Council is at present producing study-guides for a new occupational group, namely social auxiliary workers.

Population development

Apart from the functions regarding health and welfare services, the Department of National Health and Population Development is also responsible for ensuring the success of the Population Development Programme (PDP).

South Africa, like other developing countries, has a high population growth rate. The present population growth rate is 2,07% per annum. This implies that about one million people are added to the population every year. At this rate the present population will double in only 30 years' time. This is one of the most pressing problems facing the country.

In order to address the rapid population growth, the South African Government introduced the PDP in 1984. The PDP is based on international standards regarding population growth and population development. The primary goal of the PDP is to maintain a balance between population size and resources, that is, natural resources and socio-economic capabilities. In order to ensure this balance a demographic objective, namely a total fertility rate of 2,1 by the year 2010, was set. If this objective is achieved, the size of the population will stabilise at about 80 million by the end of the next century. Experts have calculated that the country can, in terms of its natural resources and socio-economic potential, only accommodate a population of that size.

The terrains on which the PDP focuses in order to reach the demographic goal are education, manpower training, primary health care (including family planning), the economy and housing. Specific programmes on these terrains have been identified. Role-players in the public as well as in the private sectors are encouraged and assisted to direct specific projects and actions on these terrains, thereby contributing to the attainment of the goal of the PDP.

Intensified information, education and communication programmes directed at changing fertility perceptions in favour of a small family norm are also launched. The aim of these programmes is to influence family size preference and fertility behaviour so that people take specific steps to achieve lower fertility levels. All possible role-players on all levels of society who can contribute are motivated to become actively involved in these programmes.

The main aim of the PDP which the Department of National Health and Population Development implemented in 1984 is to balance the size of the population and the availability of resources (natural resources and socio-economic potential). To attain this and to stabilise the population at the calculated optimum number of 80 million by the year 2100, the quality of life of all South Africans has to be enhanced. This can be achieved only by accellerating development in the fields of education, manpower training, primary health care (including family planning), housing and the economy. Internationally accepted indicators, such as the total fertility rate, infant mortality rate, teenage births and literacy are used to monitor progress. Both the public and private sectors are involved in development programmes directed at the specific fields mentioned above in order to contribute to the success of the PDP.

COMMUNITY DEVELOPMENT

Community development in South Africa is a comprehensive concept. Any state housing programme includes the provision of essential amenities such as schools, clinics, community centres, parks and recreation facilities, shopping complexes and adequate transport facilities. The object is to develop fully-fledged and self-sufficient communities with the full participation of the people concerned.

According to the Constitution, community development, which includes housing, is currently an own affair (see *Government*). Each own affairs administration has an autonomous board that controls the individual housing funds.

Housing

As a developing country, South Africa has to contend with a severe housing shortage due, among other things, to a high population growth rate (approximately 2,07% annually) and rising expectations.

In recent years the Government, in conjunction with private enterprise, has launched several new initiatives to alleviate the shortage.

Already many South Africans who can afford to do so, build or buy their own homes, usually with loans from building societies or commercial banks, or with the assistance of employers in the public and private sector.

Government initiatives
The Government is committed to a major socioeconomic programme to boost development in the residential developing communities mainly populated by black people. An amount of R3 000 million was allocated for social upliftment initiatives.

Several large state housing projects for coloured

people, such as Mitchell's Plain (250 000) and Atlantis (500 000), both near Cape Town, and for Indians (350 000) mostly in Natal, are either under construction or have been completed. The total value of Indian housing projects in 1990/91 amounted to more than R 300 million.

Major strides have been made towards attaining parity and in some cases towards bridging the gap between grants given to the different population groups. Concerted efforts are being made to address the backlog in service provision. In respect of the 1990/91 financial year, the planning of respective government department and development agencies provided for an amount of R 6 000 million for development in these areas.

Many attempts are also being made to extend private home-ownership and its mechanisms to as many South Africans as possible. In fact, in recent years in the case of blacks specifically, there has been a marked shift in housing policy — away from exclusive state responsibility in many categories to a self-help approach, that is, to build own homes according to own needs and financial capacity. This approach implies that informal residential areas are accepted. In such areas basic services are provided and residents are encouraged and assisted to upgrade the area.

The Government has accepted that if existing black residential areas are to be developed into self-sufficient communities, the residents must be given every opportunity to participate freely in the socio-economic development of such areas. The housing shortage should be eased in order also to lessen the pressure on established residential areas, to counter unlawful settling and prevent established communities from being displaced, and to protect community life from social disorder, disruption and disregard for community values. It is estimated that the population in informal settlements currently stands at seven million, with two million in the Pretoria/Witwatersrand/Vereeniging (PWV) area and 1,7 million in the Durban/Pinetown area.

The Government is also committed to the socio-economic upliftment of rural communities and the creation of opportunities to promote their entry into the mainstream of the country's development. This can be achieved through development assistance within the framework of a rural development strategy.

New policy

As a result of recent constitutional developments it became necessary to review the existing housing policy, in order to consolidate the Government's responsibilities with regard to housing on a national level.

The Government therefore commissioned the South African Housing Advisory Council to revise the present housing policy and to advise the Government on the formulation of a national housing policy, as well as a strategy to implement the policy, taking into account

— the ideal of enabling as many citizens as possible at least to own a site
— the personal responsibility of every head of a family to provide for his or his family's housing needs
— the State's responsibility to identify land for habitation
— the fact that it is financially not within the State's means to assist all citizens financially to obtain housing
— the present and foreseeable future constitutional development
— the desirability of ensuring greater involvement of the private sector in housing for the lower income groups
— the Government's policy with regard to deregulation and privatisation.

The urgent nature of the brief necessitated the appointment of the Task Group National Housing Policy and Strategy. More intensive attention is now given to the problem and to see that the formulation of possible solutions is achieved in a shorter period of time. The report of the Task Group will form the basis of a White Paper on housing which will be tabled in Parliament early in 1992.

Private sector
Security of tenure has paved the way for the private sector increasingly to enter the housing market. Today many employers help their employees to buy or build their own homes, while private property developers are opening up new residential areas and are building houses for sale to all communities.

Much of the private-sector initiative is directed through the Urban Foundation, founded and funded by large companies, either local companies or subsidiaries of foreign companies. Initially the Foundation set itself a target of R25 million in contributions. Today the Foundation has donations and funds totalling R65 million annually, as well as development capital from its own activities amounting to R250 million. Since its inception in 1977 the Foundation has launched more than

To reduce the housing backlog, people are encouraged and assisted to build their own homes

800 projects designed to upgrade the standard of living of urban black communities.

The largest ever joint-housing initiative by the State and the private sector was launched in 1986. The South African Housing Trust formed part of a package of measures announced by the Government to stimulate the South African economy. The Trust is run by prominent private-sector organisations. Funds are used for housing for low income South Africans and the general upgrading of underdeveloped residential areas.

The Independent Development Trust (IDT) was established in 1991 as a result of the process of negotiated constitutional transition. It was established specifically to address the problem of the social upliftment of the poorest sections of the community in South Africa. The IDT will initially focus its support on four development areas, namely housing, education and training, health services and community development. It intends to devote its resources to both rural and urban communities.

As far as resources are concerned, the IDT has received an initial grant amount of R2 000 million from the South African central government. These funds will all be administered independently of the State, but the IDT will be accountable to Parliament.

Land reform
In order to upgrade lower order tenure to full ownership, the Government has adopted measures to assist those with lower incomes. Provisions for regulating the proposed rationalisation of land rights and land registration systems are contained in the Upgrading of Land Tenure Rights Act.

The objective of the Government's land reform programme was to do justice to all and to broaden opportunities for all. The Abolition of Racially Based Land Measures Act which came into operation on 30 June 1991, brought an end to restrictions based on race or membership of a specific population group, and provided for the rationalisation or phasing out of cer-

As in other large cities worldwide informal settlements, brought about by increasing urbanisation, are also found in South Africa

tain racially based institutions and statutory and regulatory systems.

The Government accepts that the urbanisation process and the informal settlement phenomenon cannot be separated and accepts its responsibilities in this regard. More than 50% of the population can currently be considered urbanised. Although 10 large urban concentrations can be distinguished in South Africa, 23,2% of the entire urban population resides in the PWV area. This area comprises only 1% of the total surface area of the country.

The emphasis in dealing with informal settlers should always be on guiding these people towards land which is suitable for less formal settlement and on which at least rudimentary, but upgradable services, are available. This implies that urgent attention will have to be given to the provision and development of sufficient urban land for this purpose. Special legislation, The Less Formal Township Establishment Act provides for the establishment of legal mechanisms for the urgent provision of land suitable for settlement. Examples of informal residential areas are Orange Farm (80 000 people) near Vereeniging, Mangaung (16 000) near Bloemfontein, Duduza (24 000) near Nigel and Zonkesiswe (48 000) near Germiston.

Regional development

The deteriorating economic and socio-economic conditions made it necessary to change the approach to development in the RSA. Consequently, the emphasis moved away from national development planning to the current approach of regional development planning. Regional planning implies that all the participants in the development process are involved and the specific/-specialised needs of different communities are acknowledged on a geographical basis.

As a multidisciplinary approach, regional development is a joint priority for both the private and public sectors. The approach entails organising and directing all aspects of the human, economic and physical development in geographical areas, on the basis of development regions.

In addition to the economic objectives of continued growth and job creation, the regional approach is aimed at the optimum distribution of the population and economic activities in Southern Africa, based on the development population of regions.

Regional development comprises more than just industrial development or decentralisation. It also includes sectors such as agriculture, tourism, mining, commercial and social development, assigning to each sector its appropriate role in the development process.

Since South Africa is large and heterogeneous it cannot be regarded as a single unit for the purpose of effective planning, neither can its development be considered in isolation. The economies of the RSA (including the self-governing territories) and those of the independent states (Transkei, Bophuthatswana, Venda and Ciskei) are therefore closely integrated. Regional development is thus promoted within the context of an integrated Southern African economy and the whole area is subdivided into nine development regions, including the independent states. Within these regions a number of 'deconcentration points' (near metropolitan areas) and new 'industrial development points' (where new job opportunities will alleviate pressure on metropolitan areas) have been identified.

Structures had to be created to involve the private sector as closely as possible in the regional development process. In addition to this, development had to take place in its multilateral context without any undue advantage or disadvantage to any of the states in Southern Africa.

A new Regional Industrial Development Programme was therefore introduced in South Africa on 1 May 1991. In terms of the programme, financial incentives are offered for the establishment and expansion of manufacturing industries throughout South Africa, excluding the Durban core area and PWV area. The programme for regional industrial development forms part of a larger regional development strategy encompassing all economic sectors, which is at present being developed.

The main objective of the programme is to create wealth and employment opportunities for all South Africans in the various regions by stimulating industrial production to serve as generator of integrated economic development.

WILDLIFE AND TOURISM

Wildlife

South Africa's prolific plant and animal life is world renowned and is rated among the country's main tourist attractions.

The more than 23 000 flowering plant species is indicative of the country's abundant natural heritage. The Cape Peninsula in particular is endowed with a wealth of plant life and is regarded as one of the six floral kingdoms of the world. At the Kirstenbosch National Botanical Gardens in Cape Town, 4 000 plant species indigenous to Southern Africa are cultivated. These include the king protea, South Africa's national flower.

The country's animal kingdom includes the African

King Penguins in the National Zoological Gardens in Pretoria

elephant (world's biggest land mammal), white rhinoceros (second biggest) and hippopotamus (third), giraffe (tallest) and cheetah (fastest). Extraordinary birds include the ostrich (world's largest bird) and the kori bustard (largest flying bird).

Other species of game are the black rhinoceros, buffalo, zebra, lion, leopard, hyena and a great variety of antelope (eland, roan, sable, gemsbok, wildebeest, hartebeest, tsessebe, waterbuck, kudu, impala, reedbuck, bushbuck, nyala, duiker, oribi, steenbok, grysbok, suni, klipspringer and four species unique to South Africa: Cape grysbok, bontebok, blesbok and black wildebeest). South Africa is also home to 10% of the known species of birds and 800 species of butterflies.

There are 17 national parks, of which the largest and most popular is the Kruger National Park in the Eastern Transvaal. South Africa has an extensive variety of wild animals such as elephant, rhinoceros, lion, leopard, giraffe and what is believed to be the largest collection of antelope species in the world. The approximately 2 543 km of roads inside the park are used by 696 757 vehicles annually.

In the Kalahari Gemsbok National Park with its dry river beds, thousands of gemsbok and springbok, among others, roam free among the sparse desert shrub. The Augrabies Falls National Park preserves the creatures and plants that have adapted to the semi-desert conditions of the Northern Cape Province. The Augrabies Falls, 56 m high, is on South Africa's largest river, namely the Orange River. The outstanding feature of the Golden Gate Highlands National Park in the Northeastern Orange Free State is its breathtaking mountain scenery. In the Bontebok National Park, near Swellendam in the Western Cape Province, graceful bontebok graze in large numbers among the milkwood and wild olive trees. The rare mountain zebra, unique to South Africa, has been given sanctuary in the Mountain Zebra National Park near Cradock in the Eastern Cape Province. The Addo Elephant National Park near Port Elizabeth is a refuge for more than 160 elephants, sur-

Hout Bay, near Cape Town

vivors of the herds reduced in numbers by ivory hunters
a century or more ago. Main features of the Tsitsi-
kamma National Park are the rain forest vegetation,
including tree ferns, and rock pools filled with plant and
animal life. The Karoo and Tankwa-Karoo National
parks preserve the sparse fauna and flora of the Great
Karoo.

Several provincial and local game parks are popular
among tourists. The most important include Natal's
Hluhluwe and Umfolozi parks (the natural habitat of
the white rhinoceros. Many of these rare beasts have
been transferred to other game parks), Mkuzi, Giant's
Castle, Royal Natal and the Drakensberg Wilderness
Area; the Transvaal's Loskop Dam, Blyde River Can-

yon and Suikerbosrand; Cedarberg Wilderness Area, Hottentots-Holland Nature Reserve, De Hoop, Rolfontein and Commando Drift in the Cape Province, and the Willem Pretorius and Tussen-die-Riviere reserves in the Orange Free State. There are also numerous privately owned game parks in the Eastern Transvaal in particular.

The nature reserves and extensive wilderness areas managed by the Department of Water Affairs and Forestry are also renowned. Best known are perhaps the Ntendeka Wilderness Area (Vryheid, Natal) and the Grootbosch Nature Reserve (Magoebaskloof, Transvaal).

Tourism

In 1990, approximately 528 908 visitors from other parts of Africa visited South Africa; 48,4% of them were from Zimbabwe. Other foreign tourists totalled 498 712, 34% of them from Europe. Of the overseas tourists, 27,2% were from the United Kingdom and 16,7% came from West Germany.

South Africa's major tourist attractions include game parks and nature reserves and a magnificent scenic diversity, ranging from desert plains carpeted with spring flowers, to mountains towering above valleys and vineyards, rolling farmlands, cosmopolitan cities and traditional tribal villages (see *Population*). The coastline, nearly 3 000 km long, is dotted with sandy coves and charming seaside resorts, and includes some of the world's best bathing and surfing beaches (see *Geography*).

Other attractions include Bushman paintings, botanic gardens, bird sanctuaries, aquariums and zoos. The National Zoological Gardens in Pretoria ranks among the 10 best zoos in the world.

Daytime diversions include coach tours, ocean cruises, museums, art galleries and an extensive range of sporting opportunities. Night life encompasses the cocktail/cabaret circuit, fringe theatre and the classical performing arts. Restaurants offer Cape Malay dishes, spicy Indian curries, and French, Italian, Portuguese, Greek, German and Chinese cuisine.

The Cape wine routes are immensely popular among Capetonians and tourists alike. Among a number of other options, visitors to the Cape may also follow crayfish routes, fruit and wool routes and wild flower routes. The Northern Natal Battlefields Route has a special appeal for historians, while arts and crafts routes throughout the country attract those who love beautiful things.

Southern Africa is one of the world's most popular big game hunting destinations, offering a wide variety of trophies, including a number of rare species. Hunting seasons normally occur between 1 May and 31 July. The sport is controlled by the Professional Hunter's Association of South Africa and provincial environmental conservation bodies.

Safaris, canoeing, river rafting, wilderness trails and rambling are all part of the South African outdoor lifestyle. The popularity of hiking has been given a boost by the establishment of the National Hiking Way — a linked network of trails leading through the mountains

The Eastern Transvaal lowveld

and coastal areas of the Cape and Natal, and the escarpment area of the Eastern Transvaal.

Notable cities and towns of historical interest include Pietermaritzburg, Grahamstown, Graaff-Reinet, Port Elizabeth, Kimberley and Stellenbosch. Pilgrim's Rest, a living museum, is a replica of the mining town during the late 19th century gold rush, while Gold Reef City, in Johannesburg, is a reconstruction of the pioneer days of Johannesburg.

All of South Africa's major attractions are easily accessible by rail, road and air (see *Transport*). Efficiency is the keystone of the South African infrastructure, travel and accommodation reservations may therefore be relied upon with confidence.

Another plus factor: a perennially mild and sunny climate means that it is a pleasure to visit South Africa all year round (see *Geography*).

Accommodation standards are generally high. South Africa offers a host of country inns. The hotels are strictly graded by the South African Tourism Board according to a star allocation system. A one-star grading ranks as good; five stars indicate that the establishment is outstanding. Ungraded accommodation comprises motels, holiday flats, beach cottages, game lodges, guest farms and youth hostels. Camping/caravan parks occur throughout the country.

All South African Tourism Board offices will gladly give additional advice on all aspects of travel in South Africa. Satour has offices in the following cities:

Austria: Vienna (0943) (222) 4704-5110
Brazil: Sao Paolo (0955) (11) 259-1522
France: Paris (0933) (1) 4261-8230
Germany: Frankfurt (0949) (69) 2-0656
Israel: Tel Aviv (09972) (3) 527-2950
Italy: Milan (0939) (2) 869-3847
Japan: Tokyo (0981) (3) 478-7601
The Netherlands: Amsterdam (0931) (20) 664-6201
Republic of China: Taipei (09886) (2) 717-4238
Switzerland: Zurich (0941) (1) 715-1815
UK: London (0944) (81) 944-6646
USA: Los Angeles (091) (213) 641-8444
    New York (091) (212) 838-8841
Zimbabwe: Harare (09263) (4) 70-7766

Travel documents and other requirements
Full information is available from all Satour offices and
South African diplomatic and consular representatives
abroad. (See *Foreign Relations*.)

ENVIRONMENTAL CONSERVATION

Environmental conservation enjoys high priority in South Africa. The main objectives are the maintenance of ecological processes and systems necessary for survival, the sustainable utilisation of species and ecosystems, and the protection of the environment against deterioration as a result of human activities. These objectives and the legal measures empowering the Government to take necessary action in this regard are embodied in the Environment Conservation Act of 1989, and in a variety of other Acts and provincial ordinances.

South Africa is well known for its wealth of natural fauna and flora. These attributes are being preserved in an extensive network of official protected areas consisting of national parks, wilderness areas, provincial nature reserves and nature reserves under the control of local authorities. This system of protected areas is increased by a host of private nature reserves, conservancies and two programmes initiated by the Department of Environment Affairs, namely the SA Natural Heritage Programme and the Sites of Conservation Significance Programme. The Sites and Heritage programmes are aimed specifically at the involvement of the owners of private land in nature conservation.

Government action

In order to safeguard South Africa's environmental assets further, the voluntary execution of environmental impact assessments (EIAs) has been propagated since the early eighties. However, as many people still interpret EIA in the narrow sense, that is anti-development and not constructive, it was decided that a new term should be used in South Africa. The new term had to describe the process of guiding and documenting all

One of the successes in nature conservation in South Africa — the white rhinoceros which has been saved from extinction

development decisions to ensure the protection and wise utilisation of the environment. Integrated environmental management (IEM) was chosen.

The purpose of IEM is to ensure that environmental considerations are efficiently and adequately taken into account at all stages of the development process. IEM is concerned with all aspects and stages of environmental resource allocation, from conceptualisation, planning and assessment of possible effects, to the making and implementing of decisions and monitoring of results. It encompasses a broad range of methodologies such as terrain evaluation, ecological studies, cost-benefit analysis, social impact assessment, risk assessment, technology assessment and future research. IEM applies to all categories of proposed actions, from policy formulation to devising general programmes for effecting policies, to the initiation of specific projects. At present the implementation of IEM is being promoted actively within South Africa's development community.

In view of the problems being experienced of late in

the field of pollution control and waste management, the CSIR was commissioned by the Department of Environment Affairs to undertake a comprehensive study on this subject. The CSIR's report entitled 'The Situation of Waste Management and Pollution Control in South Africa' was published at the beginning of 1991.

This report dealt with the position of waste management and pollution control, the relevant organisations and their present actions and responsibilities in South Africa. The CSIR also reported on environmental legislation, legislative enforcement, and judgment and deficiencies in these areas. Recommendations for remedial measures were also made which should, after further discussion and consultation, find application in future environmental legislation.

A wide-ranging report containing recommendations on a national environmental management system was submitted to the Government by the President's Council in October 1991. The report calls for a steep increase in fines for industries that exceed pollution limits and suggests the closure of mines as a penalty for land damage.

Furthermore, a total restructuring of the environmental control process is recommended, with an emphasis on stricter law enforcement.

International co-operation

Since it is realised that environmental issues transcend international boundaries, South Africa is also intent upon fulfilling its international environmental responsibilities. It is an active party to various international conventions, such as the Convention on International Trade in Endangered Species of Wild Fauna and Flora (Cites) and the Convention on the Conservation of Wetlands of International Importance. South Africa is a founder member of the International Whaling Commission. Accession to the Convention on the Conservation of Migratory Fauna Species has already been approved. The Government has also decided in principle that South Africa should accede to the Basel Convention on the control of transboundary movements of hazardous wastes and their disposal. As soon as the necessary enabling amendments have been made to present legislation, South Africa will formally accede to this important convention.

As a founder member of the Antarctic Treaty, South Africa signed a protocol on the protection of the environment of Antarctica on 4 October 1991. On 21 October 1991 South Africa joined 60 countries worldwide in launching the world conservation strategy — Caring for the Earth, a Strategy for Sustainable Living. This is a joint endeavour by The World Conservation Union, the United Nations Environment Programme and the World Wide Fund for Nature (WWF). This international plan will attempt to harness all the resources of humanity to improve the global environment by measures which include massive reductions in energy consumption and the use of natural resources in industrialised countries.

Private initiatives

South African non-government organisations and particularly the Wildlife Society and the South African Nature Foundation have managed to make the South African public aware of many issues.

When there was a possibility of large-scale mining in the beautiful unspoilt St Lucia nature reserve in Natal, a petition was drawn up and signed by more than 300 000 people. A similar petition scotched plans to mine the northern Kruger National Park for coking coal in 1981. More recent activities of these organisations have resulted in the shelving of plans for the development of marinas at Robberg and St Francis Bay on the Eastern Cape coast.

Public awareness on environmental protection has been achieved by placing conservation issues on political agendas, lobbying politicians, statements in the press and the publication of booklets, reports, pamphlets and magazines. Because there was a need for suitably trained and qualified wildlife managers, the Wildlife Society raised R50 000 in 1964 to found the Chair of Wildlife Management at the University of Pretoria.

South Africa's protected areas system has been greatly enlarged as a result of the fundraising capabilities of the SA Nature Foundation (SANF). Funds raised by the SANF were used to purchase the Karoo National Park near Beaufort West and to extend the Harold Porter Botanic Garden at Betty's Bay, in the Cape Province. The Foundation has also been instrumental in negotiations for land and land swops to enlarge the West Coast, Kruger, Pilansberg and Addo Elephant National parks. The value of the land involved in these deals exceeds R100 million.

The Botanical Society was founded to support the establishment of botanic gardens in South Africa. This has culminated in the establishment of the Kirstenbosch, Drakensberg, Betty's Bay, Pietermaritzburg, Orange Free State, Lowveld and most recently the Witwatersrand Botanic Gardens.

The activities of private nature organisations also extend to other countries in Southern Africa. The auxiliary game guard system operative in the Kaokoveld, Namibia, has led to the conservation of the unique population of elephants. The programme involves the local people in the patrolling of the area and in general conservation work and now also serves as an example to others. This project was mainly financed by the Endangered Wildlife Trust.

In the field of formal environmental education the private sector has also played a leading role. Under the protection of the Wildlife Society the Umgeni Valley Ranch Environmental Education Programme, the first of its kind, commenced in Natal in 1975. From this project has flowed resource material and ideas for teaching, using the environment. Between 20 000 and 30 000 school children visit Umgeni Valley each year and many other environmental education schools, modelled on this project, have started up round the country.

In the adult education sector the activities of the Wilderness Leadership School have played a major role in awakening commitment to the environment by decision-makers in business and other sectors of the economy. Often the decisions of these people can have a dramatic effect on the environment through pollution, for example, when the environment is not considered in their thinking.

Private nature organisations have undertaken or funded many research projects that supplied information which could be acted on. The Endangered Wildlife Trust has funded projects for the conservation of the Blue Swallow, Pangolin, Red and Blue Duiker, Roan Antelope, Cheetah, Black Rhino and Dolphins. The Dolphin Action and Protection Group has run a number of campaigns which have resulted in the banning of further Dolphinarium construction and the capture of dolphins off South Africa's coast, and heavy fines for fishing boats carrying gillnets in its coastal waters.

The Wildlife Society's Ozone Campaign, which saw the institution of an 'Ozone-friendly' logo, raised public awareness of stratospheric ozone depletion and has resulted in the rapid phasing out of CFC products used in aerosol cans. The National Committee to Coordinate Recycling has increased awareness of the need for recycling and developed the necessary structures for this to be implemented practically.

SPORT

South African sportsmen and women continue to excel on the playing fields of the world and at home, establishing new world and South African records and scoring remarkable feats. One of the reasons is probably South Africa's ideal climate which permits all forms of outdoor sport and recreation to be enjoyed virtually throughout the year in most parts of the country.

Non-racial competition in individual and team sports has become commonplace. Sports teams, individual participants and representatives of controlling bodies are selected on merit at club, provincial (regional) and national level.

The nineties has heralded a new phase for sport in South Africa due to the fact that South Africans are increasingly being allowed to participate in international competitions once again.

This has been made possible through the favourable political developments that have taken place in the country since 2 February 1990.

The sports moratorium

The sports moratorium on international tours came under discussion, particularly during Mike Gatting's English cricket tour of South Africa in 1990. One of the main reasons given by the National and Olympic Sports Congress (NOSC) for the introduction of a sports moratorium, is that money spent on international tours should rather be spent on the upliftment of the disadvantaged in South Africa. It is maintained further that international tours cannot be permitted as long as South African sports bodies remain divided in their own ranks.

The Government's standpoint in this regard is clear: all forms of sanctions against South Africa, thus also the sports moratorium, must be ended. The Government could not identify itself with the sports moratorium, because it was on an open agenda with no clarity on who would lift it, how long it would last and under what conditions it would be lifted. Meanwhile, these questions were discussed by the International Olympic Committee (IOC) during its visit to South Africa. It was stated clearly that the IOC alone would decide on the lifting of the sports moratorium. Notwithstanding this decision, the National Olympic Committee of South Africa (NOCSA) decided to leave the final authority regarding the lifting of the sports moratorium in the hands of the ANC-controlled NOSC and the South African Non-Racial Olympic Committee (SANROC).

Sport bodies

South African National Olympic Committee (SANOC)
Since South Africa was denied participation in the Olympic Games in 1964 and the country's membership of the IOC was ended in 1970, the main aim of SANOC has been to strive to have South Africa readmitted to the Olympic Games. SANOC has 41 affiliated national sports bodies, some of which represent non-Olympic sports.

In 1990 SANOC founded a five-man working committee in conjunction with the NOSC, and SANROC. The aim of this committee was to establish a single Olympic movement for South African sport.

SANOC was a strong supporter of the sports moratorium which formed part of the reasons for the dissension between SANOC and the other traditional sports umbrella body, the Confederation of South African Sport (COSAS).

Confederation of South African Sport (COSAS)
The establishment of COSAS in March 1989 was the result of years of investigation into the rationalisation of macro sport in the RSA. It stems from the former South African Sports Federation which was established in 1953. COSAS is the most representative macro sports umbrella body in the country with 141 sports organisations affiliated to it.

In contrast to SANOC, COSAS is opposed to the moratorium, but it is also not in favour of so-called 'rebel tours'. COSAS is of the opinion that opposition sports groups are not aiming at power-sharing, but at the complete take-over of the sports set-up in the RSA.

National and Olympic Sports Congress (NOSC)
The NOSC was officially launched in Cape Town on 1 July 1990. Approximately 22 sports bodies are affiliated to the NOSC. It enjoys the official support of various political organisations to the left of the political spectrum, such as the ANC, Cosatu and the Mass Democratic Movement.

South African Council on Sport (SACOS)
SACOS was founded in 1973 and became well known for its slogan: 'No normal sport in an abnormal society'. SACOS represents about 18 so-called 'non-racial' sports bodies. Before the establishment of the NOSC, SACOS was the main internal organisation that promoted 'non-racial' sport in the RSA. Since its foundation SACOS has not had the ability to provide actual sports services to its members, who consist mainly of Indians and coloureds. Until the late 1980s SACOS enjoyed close links with SANROC, which was based in London, but the relationship has since become strained.

National Olympic Committee of South Africa (NOCSA)
Talks on the future of South African sport took place in Harare, Zimbabwe on 3 and 4 November 1990. The two most important decisions taken were the following:

The sports boycott against South Africa must be maintained until apartheid is totally eliminated and a single controlling body for South African sport must be created.

The announced Committee of Ten (comprising two members from each of the five nominated umbrella bodies) have to work towards this. The Committee of Ten, later also known as the South African Coordinating Committee (SACC) under the chairmanship of Mr

Sam Ramsamy of SANROC held three meetings during January and February 1991 before reporting to a Monitoring Committee of the Association of National Olympic Committees of Africa (ANOCA) in Gaberone on 9 and 10 March 1991. The SACC was renamed the Interim National Olympic Committee of South Africa (INOCSA) in Gaberone. According to reports, INOCSA insisted that all sports controlling bodies in South Africa had to be disbanded and that they had to affiliate with INOCSA, which would then strive towards obtaining international recognition for the sports bodies. Since the re-acceptance of South Africa as a full member of the IOC on 9 July 1991, INOCSA became a permanent structure referred to as NOCSA.

International community

Several international sports organisations, of which the IOC is the most important, have made it clear that they are in favour of South Africa's return to world sport. This was confirmed when the official IOC delegation which visited South Africa from 23 to 27 March 1991, announced at a news conference that South Africa would be conditionally readmitted to the IOC. The five conditions set for South Africa's full-fledged membership of the IOC were as follows:

— The scrapping of apartheid.
— The structure and actions of INOCSA must comply with the Olympic Charter.
— INOCSA must move towards the establishment of a permanent Olympic movement for South Africa and strive for the normalisation of sports relations.
— The achievement of unity in sport on a non-racial basis.
— INOCSA must work for the normalisation of relations with international sports bodies such as the ANOCA.

Until these requirements are met, the sports moratorium must be maintained.

In a further step the vice-president of the IOC and

leader of the delegation to South Africa, Judge Keba Mbaye, announced at an IOC Board meeting in Barcelona on 15 April 1991 that the chances of South Africa being invited to take part in the 1992 winter and summer Olympic Games were good. The IOC also granted two million dollars for the upliftment of sport in South Africa.

During President de Klerk's visits to Europe, several heads of state expressed themselves in favour of resuming sporting ties with South Africa. The announcement of the United Nations' Special Committee Against Apartheid on 24 April 1991 that the names of international sports coaches would no longer be put on the blacklist in future and that the list as such would possibly be scrapped, is further proof that South Africa's sporting isolation is coming to an end.

European Community leaders said in a draft communique at their meeting in Luxembourg on 29 June 1991 that they were in favour of renewing sporting contacts with South Africa because of the 'important progress' that has been made in abolishing apartheid.

To return to the Olympics is the greatest sports bonanza South Africa could have hoped for — and without the ending of apartheid it would not have happened.

South Africa's return to the IOC was now inevitable. The isolation that kept South Africa out for 21 years after its expulsion in 1970 ended on 9 July 1991, when South Africa was readmitted to the IOC. This return was confirmed in an official letter to SANOC on 15 July 1991.

On 25 July 1991 the IOC issued official invitations to 167 nations to compete in the summer Olympic Games in Barcelona and after two decades of isolation, South Africa was among those invited.

The Olympic Charter demands at least five national sports federations be affiliated to a country's national Olympic committee. Judge Keba Mbaye, the IOC's vice-president, said he understood that thus far 11 had achieved racial unity.

On 6 November 1991 the chairman of NOCSA, Mr

Sam Ramsamy, announced that NOCSA would accept an invitation from the IOC to participate in the Olympic Games in Barcelona in 1992. Mr Ramsamy said the mechanics of participation at Barcelona for many NOCSA affiliates would be a matter between individuals and their international bodies.

Achievements

In most of the major sports, players and officials of all races have come into their own. In athletics 5 000 black athletes regularly take part in events at all levels. There are 2 000 qualified black officials and about 500 coaches.

In 1991 Elana Meyer and Zola (Budd) Pieterse set the best times in the world for the 3 000 m since the Olympics of 1988.

Brian Mitchell, the WBA junior lightweight boxing champion, has successfully defended his title 12 times. On 14 September 1991 Brian Mitchell also became the IBF junior lightweight champion of the world when he convincingly defeated Tony Lopez of the USA. Welcome Ncita of South Africa retained his IBF junior featherweight title by defeating the Colombian, Sugar Baby Rojas, on 28 September 1991.

In 1987 Kevin Flanegan won the annual marathon race at Marathon, Greece. In 1989 Bruce Fordyce and Frith van der Merwe established themselves as two of the world's best ultramarathon athletes. Fordyce duly won an international 100 km race at Stellenbosch, breaking the official world best with a time of 6:25:07. In the process he beat the best ultra-racers in the world — among them world champion Domingo Catalan of Spain. In 1990 Fordyce won the gruelling Comrades road race for a record ninth time.

Rugby is the major national winter sport. The Springboks have a proud international record, but owing to political pressure there have been progressively fewer tours abroad by South African rugby sides. However, both official and unofficial international sides have continued to tour South Africa. In 1986, an 'unofficial' All Black side was beaten 3-1 by the Springboks in a four match series. The All Blacks were followed by the South Sea Barbarians in 1987. The South African Barbarians won the 'test series' 2-0.

In 1988 the Nampak SA Pioneers went to South America, where they wore jerseys in three colours which represented the various units that formed the SA Rugby Board — green for Springboks, black for the Leopards (SA Rugby Association) and gold for the Proteas (SA Rugby Federation). This was the first senior team of the SA Rugby Board to tour abroad since 1981. They beat Chile 100-6 and Paraquay 100-4.

In 1989 the FNB International rugby team played two tests against the Springboks as part of the centenary of the SA Rugby Board and lost 2-0 to Jannie Breedt's SA team.

Four South African rugby players were included in the team of the Barbarians who played against Scotland on 7 September 1991.

At present rugby in the RSA is managed by two separate umbrella bodies — the largest and most representative body is the South African Rugby Board of Dr Danie Craven and a lesser body the South African Rugby Union of Mr Ebrahim Patel.

South Africa was a founder member of the International Lawn Tennis Federation (now the International Tennis Federation). By winning both the Federation Cup in 1972 (Brenda Kirk, Greta Delport and Pat Pretorius) and the Davis Cup in 1974 (Bob Hewitt, Frew McMillan, Cliff Drysdale, Byron Bertram, Ray Moore and Robert Maud), South Africa joined a small, elite band in the international tennis fold.

Frew McMillan and Bob Hewitt won the men's doubles at Wimbledon in 1967, 1972 and 1978, and Bob Hewitt and Greer Stevens the mixed doubles in 1977. Kevin Curren and Yvonne Vermaak both reached the semi-finals of the singles in 1983 and Curren became the first South African to reach the finals in the singles in 1984, eliminating Jimmy Connors and John McEnroe, two former Wimbledon champions, on his way to the final.

In 1989 Danie Visser and Pieter Aldrich won the USA men's doubles in Indianapolis, USA.

In October 1991 it was announced that the sports moratorium on international tennis participation was lifted and that the International Tennis Federation had decided to stage the World's Doubles Championships in South Africa during November 1991.

In golf Gary Player established himself as one of the greatest players of all time. He has won more than 150 major titles in the world of golf: the British Open (in 1959, 1968 and 1974), the American Open (in 1965), the American Masters (in 1961, 1974 and 1978) and the American PGA (in 1962 and 1972) among others. This has made him one of only three players in golfing history to win all four of the so-called 'Big Ones' or 'Grand Slam' tournaments. In 1988 Player won the USA PGA Masters, Florida Masters, British Open Masters and the USA Masters, for yet another Masters 'Grand Slam'. In the last three years Mark McNulty (on the European tour: Portuguese Open, 1986; British Masters, West German Open, 1987, 1991), David Frost (USA tour — Tuscon Open, 1988; World Series of Golf in 1989) and Nick Price (South Australian Open in 1989; Byron Nelson Open) were South Africa's best golf players. McNulty (1988) and Frost (1989-1990) won the Million Dollar tournament at Sun City defeating some of the world's best golfers.

There has been no official competition in cricket since 1970-71 when the Springboks beat Australia 4-0 in the test series played in South Africa. However, in 1982 the South Africans beat unofficial sides from England and Sri Lanka, and early in 1983 an unofficial side from the West Indies. In 1983/84 another West Indian team toured South Africa. The Springboks also beat unofficial representative sides from Australia in 1985/86 and in 1986/87. In 1990 a cricket tour by an unofficial side from England was called off due to political pressure.

Equal opportunities are available to all who wish to

play cricket. Merit selection is the only criterium used when selecting players.

A non-racial development programme is extremely costly and the funds come mainly from the newly formed United Cricket Board of South Africa and the business community. This generous sponsorship enabled about 50 000 disadvantaged youngsters to participate in cricket programmes during 1989.

Cricket is played in black communities throughout the year in many parts of South Africa. Many youngsters have graduated from soft-ball, mini cricket to the hard-ball version of the game and encouraging advances have been made. The development programme for black communities has created an enormous demand for coaching and facilities. It requires the services of full-time cricketers to overcome the difficulties of coaching, transport, facilities and communications.

The Cricket Coaching Academy has played a major role in coordinating the development of cricket at all levels, including cricket in black towns, and the training of coaches. They now have more than 2 600 registered coaches of whom more than 800 are active.

In the past three years several South Africans, such as the Springboks Jimmy Cook and Alan Donald, have done very well in English county cricket. Cook was one of Wisden's Five Cricketers of the Year in 1989. Clive Rice, captain of the 1986/87 South African cricket side, has three times been named the world's best all-round cricketer — in 1984, 1985 and 1987.

The game that attracts the most spectators is football (soccer). All players are selected on merit, regardless of race.

Of the 300 000 netball players at least 200 000 are blacks, coloureds and Indians. Black cyclists regularly take part in the annual international Rapport Tour.

South African sports administrators serve on international bodies. Judge H W O Klopper (1982) was chairman of the World Boxing Association, Prof Fritz Eloff (1990) chairman of the World Rugby Board and Mr Steve Strydom (1985) was the first South African referee to officiate in the Five Nations rugby series in Europe. Mr Strydom was followed by Fransie Muller (1988), Freek Burger (1990) and Albert Adams (1991).

Progress in sport organisation

Agreement was reached on all the 'salient points' to be incorporated in a draft constitution, following a meeting of the National Rugby Steering Committee at Newlands on 23 March 1991. The Committee also reaffirmed its commitment to establish a single National Controlling Body for rugby in South Africa. All controlling bodies of SA rugby will disband to form one controlling body: the South African Rugby Football Union (SARFU).

South African ice hockey was welcomed backed into the international arena on 3 May 1991.

In 1991 South Africa celebrated its return to international cricket with a tour to India. Kepler Wessels (left) and Sanjay Manjrekar shared the Man of the Series Award

South Africa's 21-year absence from world cricket ended at the sport's traditional headquarters at Lord's on 10 July 1991.

'This inaugural meeting of the United Cricket Board of South Africa (UCBSA) is another clear indication that goodwill among people will always triumph,' the managing director of the UCBSA said in his inaugural address in Johannesburg on 29 June 1991.

South Africa's return to the international arena was announced by Colin Cowdrey, Chairman of the International Cricket Council (ICC), the game's world ruling authority.

Mr Cowdrey said the ICC recognised the new body for cricket in South Africa, namely the United Cricket Board of South Africa (UCBSA), and elected them to full membership 'with immediate effect'.

On 23 October 1991 South Africa's application to play in the Benson & Hedges World Cup Cricket Tournament in Australia and New Zealand in 1992 was approved.

A South African cricket side captained by Clive Rice left for India to play three one-day internationals in November 1991. This was South Africa's first official international cricket competition since the country was isolated in 1970.

South Africa's readmission to international soccer remains at least a year away, Mr Guido Tognoni, a FIFA spokesman, said on 10 July 1991 at the sport's head office in Zurich. According to him, South Africa's readmission to the IOC would not expedite FIFA's timetable for a decision to lift its 15-year-old ban.

On 17 July 1991 Mr Issa Hayatou, President of the Confederation of African Football (CAF), said on his arrival in Johannesburg that 'member countries belonging to the CAF, the ruling body in Africa, would welcome a fully integrated South Africa back into its organisation with open arms'.

'The recent political initiatives of President de Klerk paved the way for the CAF visit,' he said.

On 11 August 1991 total unity in SA soccer was

achieved at a historic meeting between the SA Football Association (SAFA) and the SA National Football Association (SANFA).

In spite of the unification in South African soccer, CAF did not approve South Africa's membership during a members meeting in September 1991.

On 12 July 1991 South African surfing received the gratifying news that its membership of the international body had been fully restored.

South African cycling was welcomed back in the international arena, Mr Gotty Hansen, senior vice-president of the SA Cycling Federation (SACF), announced on 15 July 1991 after it had been accepted as a full member by the executive of the FIAC at its congress in Colorado Springs.

On 19 July 1991 the World Boxing Organisation (WBO) decided by unanimous vote to sanction world title fights in South Africa. 'Many doors would open to South African amateur boxers following the unity achieved on 13 July 1991,' Colonel Soon Pretorius, president of the new South African National Boxing Organisation (SANABO), said. He was elected the first president of SANABO.

South African table tennis was united on 21 July 1991, and since then the new body has been given assurances of early assistance from overseas bodies and the prospects of playing in international events. The SA Table Tennis Board and the SA Table Tennis Union were merged into a new body, the SA Table Tennis Board (SATTB), and immediately applied for affiliation to NOCSA.

Mr Menzo Barrish, General Manager of the South African Association for the Disabled (SAAD), announced on 23 July 1991 that his association had been readmitted to the International Federation. There has been unity in the SAAD since 1974.

On 25 July 1991 the South African Judo Union was given official recognition by the African Judo Union and the International Judo Federation, and granted full membership. Two South Africans, Marvin Mesias and

Leslie Stoch, were allowed to take part as delegates in the international judo congress held in Barcelona.

It was agreed on 29 July 1991 that the SA Golf Association (SAGA) of Mr Henry Govender and the SA Golf Union (SAGU) of Mr Mike Watermeyer should continue unity talks.

Unity in squash is a mere formality and South Africa will host the 1992 world championships, following the announcement by the International Squash Players Association (ISPA) on 5 August 1991 that South Africa had been chosen to host the 1992 championships. The last major ISPA-sanctioned tournament to be held in South Africa was the 1973 World individual and team championships.

On 1 August 1991 South African canoeing was readmitted to the International Canoeing Federation after being expelled in 1970.

'The International Tennis Federation (ITF) would like to readmit South Africa as soon as possible,' Mr Brian Tobin, president of the ITF said on his arrival in Johannesburg on 11 August 1991 as head of a fact-finding delegation 'to encourage the three groups (SA Tennis Union, Tennis Federation of SA and Tennis Association of SA) to mould into a fully integrated and united body'. Since then a unified body, Tennis South Africa, emerged with Mr Chris Ngcobo the new chairman.

On 20 August 1991, Mr As Burger, honorary chairman of the International Union of Modern Pentathlon and Biathlon (IUMPB) put South Africa's case to the annual congress of the IUMPB as a result of which the South African Modern Pentathlon Association (SAMPA) has been welcomed back. SAMPA's membership of the IUMPB has never been suspended, but for various reasons modern pentathlon teams have not competed at international level during the eighties.

In September 1991 the Springbok gymnastic team participated in the world championships in Indianapolis, USA.

On 26 August 1991 the South African Yacht Racing

Association (SAYRA) was granted membership of NOCSA — and participation in the 1992 Barcelona Games is now a reality.

The SA Hockey and the SA Men's Hockey Association held unity talks in Cape Town and in a statement they confirmed that both bodies had found the necessary common purpose and would continue talks after reporting to their constituent bodies.

The sports moratorium was lifted on 24 August 1991 for professional golf, amateur boxing, road running and the *tae kwon do* martial arts and the NOSC also gave cricket qualified approval.

The barriers facing other integrated sports will fall in time.

South Africa's sportsmen and women will once more be successful in the world of sport. For all those who are participating in Olympic sports — the athletes, the wrestlers, the boxers, the soccer players, the horse jumpers and others — the chance at last to compete in the Olympics is a dream come true.

Regional offices of the South African Communication Service (SACS)

The Regional Representative
SA Communication Service
Private Bag X20500
93000 BLOEMFONTEIN
Tel: (051) 48-4504/5/6

The Regional Representative
SA Communication Service
Private Bag X9007
8000 CAPE TOWN
Tel: (021) 21-5070

The Regional Representative
SA Communication Service
Private Bag X54332
4000 DURBAN
Tel: (031)301-6787/8/9

The Regional Representative
SA Communication Service
Private Bag X16
2000 JOHANNESBURG
Tel: (011) 337-3120 to 9

The Regional Representative
SA Communication Service
Private Bag X6061
6000 PORT ELIZABETH
Tel: (041) 55-9141

The Regional Representative
SA Communication Service
Private Bag X410
0001 PRETORIA
Tel: (012) 342-2780/1/2

The Regional Representative
SA Communication Service
PO Box 327
6280 GRAAFF-REINET
Tel: (0491) 2-2123/4

The Regional Representative
SA Communication Service
PO Box 726
5200 EAST LONDON
Tel: (0431) 43-2574

The Regional Representative
SA Communication Service
Private Bag X9326
0700 PIETERSBURG
Tel: (01521) 91-2045

The Regional Representative
SA Communication Service
Private Bag X11288
1200 NELSPRUIT
Tel: (01311) 2-8311

Editing and layout: Minette Pietersen
Sub-editing: Diana Coetzee
Artwork: Karen van der Merwe

Published by the
South African Communication Service,
Private Bag X745, Pretoria 0001.
Printed and bound
for the Government Printer, Pretoria,
by CTP Book Printers, Parow,
January 1992

ISBN 0 7970 2391 7